CW00518423

The Nervous Nineties

Pioneer of Test 99 Club, Aussie great Clem Hill scored 99, 98 and 97 in consecutive Test innings in 1902. (Ken Piesse library)

The Nervous Nineties

Kersi Meher-Homji

Foreword by Michael Slater

Kangaroo Press

To my sons Jehangir and Zubin

Cover design by Darian Causby.
Cover photo: Michael Atherton, crawling on hands and
knees, watches Ian Healy shatter the stumps, as the dejected
England opener is run out for 99. (Patrick Eagar)

© Kersi Meher-Homji

First published in 1994 by Kangaroo Press Pty Ltd
3 Whitehall Road Kenthurst NSW 2156 Australia
PO Box 6125 Dural Delivery Centre NSW 2158
Printed by Australian Print Group, Maryborough VIC 3465

ISBN 0 86417 650 3

Contents

Foreword

It seems appropriate that the quirky cricket-writer Kersi Meher-Homji has penned his unique *The Nervous Nineties* in the mid-1990s, the decade of uncertainty, recession and a hesitant recovery.

This decade has been a big one for milestones in cricket: the introduction of Zimbabwe to Test cricket; the welcome return of South Africa to the Test fold with apartheid dismantled; and records set by Allan Border, Sir Richard Hadlee, Kapil Dev and Brian Lara.

The Nervous Nineties is focused on the trauma, drama, humour and statistics of batsmen dismissed in their nineties. Having gone through the anguish of three nineties (it could have been four) within nine Tests and four months, I know too well what it feels like to be out when a few runs short of a century.

I will never forget the awesome feeling, not only of disappointment but also of total disbelief, at being dismissed for 99 against New Zealand in Perth last season. Before that fateful delivery from Dipak Patel, getting out was the last thing on my mind. I felt invincible at that stage of my innings and knew that all my concentration and hard work would be rewarded with just one run.

However, disaster struck. Patel managed to turn one down leg side quite sharply and in my excitement I tried to turn it fine for a single, but somehow only managed to glove it straight to the keeper. I turned very slowly to view the umpire, hoping he didn't think I had hit it, but the sight of his raised finger haunts me as much today as it did that evening.

I put my hand on my head in sheer disbelief and then realised I had to depart the arena, unable to comprehend how it could have happened.

Lightning nearly struck again in my very next Test innings at Hobart. To say I felt nervous on 99 this time would be an understatement. I could not stop thinking about Perth and, with Patel bowling again, there certainly was a distinct feeling of déjà vu.

With irrational thoughts dominating, I pushed the next ball to mid-on and called Boony (David Boon) for a single. He was startled by the ridiculous call and in an attempt to set off quickly he lost his footing, slipped over and sent me diving back for the crease.

Fortunately, luck was with me. I survived the run out appeal and went on to score 168. Had I been adjudged run out, I would have become the first batsman to score 99s in successive Test innings in 118 years of Test cricket, this book informs me. I've a sneaking suspicion that Kersi wanted me to be given run out at 99 in Hobart just to 'spice up' his book!

Seriously, I was so relieved to see the three-figures going up on the scoreboard against my name. It was only intense nervousness which made me even attempt that single (when on 99) which very nearly made me come unstuck in Hobart.

Anyway, I provided Kersi with more material (he calls it 'inspiration') for his book by scoring 92 in the Sydney Test and 95 in Durban—both in 1994. Still, I am far from being a record-holder. The West Indies left-hander Alvin Kallicharran beats me hands down, having made eight nineties (in 66 Tests), Kersi tells me. Well, this is one record I don't want to break. It may be good for the soul, but it's not so hot for the ticker!

Although Kersi is frequently referred to in Column 8 of the *Sydney Morning Herald* as indefatigable, he at times appears a bit sadistic to me! When he is not digging out records of batsmen making seven ducks in a row, he is unearthing stories of a cricketer making 99 in both innings of a match, or those getting run out for 99 without the consolation of a later century, or those robbed of their hundreds by rain, cruel declarations by their captain, the pitch being dug up by vandals, riots...once even by contracting measles. Measles at 99?

And I thought *I* was unlucky in Perth!

Apart from the legendary Clem Hill getting out for 99, 98 and 97 in successive Test innings in 1902, the Sob Story of the Century Award should go to an Aussie Test debutant Arthur Chipperfield. I'll let you read all about it.

All in all, *The Nervous Nineties* is a delightful read. Strong in stats (giving records the all-knowing *Wisden* bypasses), the book is replete with beaut little anecdotes at Test, first-class and junior levels—most of them previously unpublished. Kersi has done in-depth research to give the correct version of how and why Hanif Mohammad was run out for 499.

This publication should appeal as much to active cricketers and cricket buffs as to those only mildly interested in the game.

Michael Slater
June, 1994

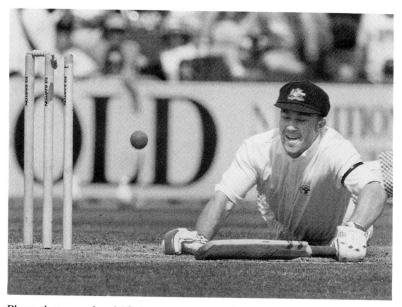

Phew, that was close! 'Only nervousness, when on 99, made me go for that impossible single,' recalled Michael Slater. He narrowly escaped and scored 168 in the 1993 Hobart Test. (Mark Baker, *Reuters*)

Acknowledgments

If I were to place all those who helped me with the book end-on-end, they would probably reach the top of Centre Point Tower. Even higher, some of them are pretty tall!

Firstly, my thanks to Michael Slater, not only for his entertaining Foreword, but also for indirectly giving me the idea of this book. His dismissal for 99 in the Perth Test in November 1993 (with myriad replays on Channel 9), then nearly running himself out for 99 in his next Test innings at Hobart, followed by his 90s in the Sydney and Durban Tests, is the inspiration behind the book.

Thanks also to my statistician friends for checking some of my data and providing more. They are: Bapoo Mama, Ross Dundas (who supplied the nineties in limited-overs matches list), Dr Colin Clowes (who gave me the rare information on batsmen who remained unbeaten in the nineties at stumps, wondering and fearing what the morrow would bring), Dr Vasant Naik, Shahzad Ali Khan and Sudhir Vaidya. David Baggett's and Robert Brooke's in-depth research on 99s in first-class cricket, as published in *The Cricket Statistician* (England), was invaluable. So was Kanti Suthar's research on 99-run partnerships as published in *Anka* (India). And thank you, Qamar Ahmed, for interviewing Hanif Mohammad for me and getting the correct version of how Hanif was run out for 499 in 1959.

When in need, cricket-lovers Norman Halpin, Warwick Franks and Vasant Raiji rallied round, as did my mates at the NSW Cricket Association Library, Stephen Gibbs and Jack McHarg. I am grateful to first-class umpires Graham Reed and Arthur Watson, and cricketers Michael Whitney, Michael Slater, Alan Davidson, Rusi Surti, Kerry O'Keeffe and Gavin Robertson for sharing with me their nervous nineties stories.

Then there were the readers of the *Sydney Morning Herald*, *Inside Edge*, *Cricketer* (Australia) and *Wisden Cricket Monthly* (England) who responded to my appeal for their tragi-comic experiences. My thanks to the following whose stories are used: David Frith and L.H. Coulson from England; Nigel Smith from New Zealand; Graham Clayton, Peter Terrey, Frank Ryan, John Hook, Kingsley Alley, Marc Dawson, Keith Ross, Graeme White, David Bridge and Jack Brown from NSW; Clarrie Sutton from Queensland and Brett Day from South Australia.

Articles by Gerald Brodribb (*The Cricketer*, England, 13 May 1950), M.S. Rogers and Irving Rosenwater (*The Cricketer Spring Annual 1959*), Simon R. Wilde (*Cricket Quarterly*, Pakistan, 1978–79), B.B. Mama (*Sportsweek*, India, 5 October 1983), Syed Rizwan Akhter (*World of Cricket*, Pakistan, May 1985) and editor (*Wisden Cricket Monthly*, England, June 1991) were essential for the kaleidoscopic information within.

My grateful thanks to Peter Christopher and Andrew Foulds from the *Sydney Morning Herald,* Ken Piesse, Patrick Eagar, Mark Baker from Reuters, Rusi Surti and Jack Pollard for the supply of pictures, to Tony Rafty for the cartoon and to David Chaves for the graphics.

The following authors are quoted: Colin Cowdrey from *MCC: The Autobiography of a Cricketer* (Hodder & Stoughton, 1976), Bob Simpson from *Captain's Story* (Marlin Books, Hutchinson Group, 1977), Dudley Nourse from *Cricket in the Blood* (Hodder & Stoughton, 1949), Geoff Boycott from *Boycott: The Autobiography* (Macmillan, 1987), Mike Whitney from *Quick Whit: The Mike Whitney Story* (Ironbark, Pan Macmillan, 1993), Jack Pollard from *Australian Cricket: The Game and the Players* (Hodder & Stoughton, 1982), Marc Dawson from *The Bumper Book of Cricket Extras* (Kangaroo Press, 1993), Frank Tyson from *The Century Makers: The Men Behind the Ashes 1877–1977* (Hutchinson, 1980), Rod Marsh from *You'll Keep* (Hutchinson, 1975), Steve Waugh from *Steve Waugh's Ashes Diary* (Ironbark, Pan Macmillan, 1993), Jonathan Rice from *Curiosities of Cricket* (Pavilion, 1993), Gordon Greenidge from *Gordon Greenidge: The Man in the Middle* (David & Charles, 1980) and Phill Cartwright from *90+: A Study of Scores of 90–99* (Roit Productions, 1991).

Books and periodicals to which I have referred include *Wisden Cricketers' Almanac* (several issues), *The Wisden Book of Test Cricket 1876–77 to 1977–78* and *The Wisden Book of Cricket Records* (both compiled and edited by Bill Frindall), *The Concise Wisden: An Illustrated Anthology of 125 Years* (edited by Benny Green, 1990),

Figures of Cricket by Sudhir Vaidya, *The Complete Book of Australian Test Cricket Records* by Ross Dundas and Jack Pollard, several issues of *The Cricket Statistician* (England)—especially numbers 68, 70, 71 and 78 (edited by Philip Bailey), *Wisden Cricket Monthly* (England) edited by David Frith, and *Cricketer* (Australia) edited by Ken Piesse.

Finally, a big thank you to David Rosenberg, the publisher of Kangaroo Press, to the editor, Carl Harrison-Ford, and to Tricia Ritchings for her word-processing skills and patience in excelsis to accommodate my second, third and fourth thoughts.

Introduction

Send me no flowers
Just a stiff drink will do
And a couple of dry hankies
I'm in the nervous nineties.

You have smashed bowlers all over the ground without a care. But suddenly the throat dries up and the same bowlers appear like Larwood, Laker, Lillee and Warne rolled into one. Grass grows instantly on the pitch, the ball shrinks in size and starts reverse-swinging, the fielders get so close you can sniff their aftershave and the friendly crowd turns deliriously diabolical.

You are in the nervous nineties, right?

You take fresh guard, request drinks, a new pair of gloves and a couple of desiccated hankies. The anxiety climaxes to 'nonagenarian's neurosis' as you climb—or rather totter—to 99. Then only luck takes you to the ultimate: a century.

Many more centuries have been scored (over 2000) than 99s (only 50) in 118 years of Test cricket. Often these 99ers are remembered more than the centurions, but as six of them have never managed a Test hundred, we can well imagine their chagrin.

Although only one run separates 99 from 100 the difference is HUGE to the batsmen, the spectators and the statisticians. Like setting a foot on the summit of Everest or being gobbled up by a Yeti a metre below the pinnacle. Or a marathon runner collapsing a centimetre short of the finishing line.

If tennis great Ivan Lendl was a cricketer he would have scored 99 every time at Lord's.

Scholars have debated for long as to what is more tragic: to be out for a duck or to be dismissed in the nineties. If cricket were popular in Russia, there would have been mega-novels not climaxed by three characters hanging themselves and four stabbing others, but by three sad Cossacks making ducks and four scoring 99s.

Then we could have drawn some conclusions. Unfortunately, no such literary work exists. Having written *Out for a Duck* in 1993—detailing all the traumas and dramas of non-scoring—without suffering a nervous breakdown, I now undertake this tear-jerker with confidence. Not all the nineties in the book are nervous; some are philosophical, some gallant, others weird. But they all have at least a tinge of pathos—a feeling of failure to achieve even after achieving.

To misquote John Greenleaf Whittier:

> For all sad words of tongue or pen,
> The saddest are these:
> 'It might have been—
> A century!'

Traditionally, a century has a special aura about it. It is often the yardstick by which batsmen are ultimately judged. And yet, is a 90, 96 or 99 any less of an achievement? At best, a ninety is a bronze medal, at worst—a heart-wrenching experience.

Some critics had stated that my *Out for a Duck* was too specialised—harping on ducks, only ducks and nothing but the ducks. I have thwarted them in the current cri-gedy (cricket tragedy) which includes emotional and statistical aspects of batsmen scoring from 90 to 99, as also 199, 299 and 499 in an innings.

Now read on, but don't forget the tissues.

1 My Vicarious Anguish

To be dismissed in the nineties is always regarded as
'unlucky' in that the man has missed a distinction
which he has earned.

—Gerald Brodribb

I may as well come out in the open. A tail-end batsman, my highest
score is 42, not even half of 90. So what qualifications do I have to
write a book on nervous nineties?

I can imagine a disgruntled batsman (embittered by a few scores of
ninety) confronting me with 'And what would *you* know about the
heartache of a 90?'

My answer is ready. I may not be a cat but I exactly know what
Tom goes through living with Jerry—just the type of creature to stump
or run out an unsuspecting batsman for 99.

Also, you don't have to be an ox to be the best judge of steak
diane.

Back to cricket. Without actually suffering the trauma of a ninety
myself, I have borne the vicarious torture of a just-missed century or
a painfully lingering ninety. The nearest I came to a personal feeling
of acute anxiety and mental anguish of a nervous ninety was during
the Sydney Test of January 1982.

John Dyson, the stodgy Australian batsman playing his maiden
Test against the West Indies, was the crowd hero by taking a spectacular
catch in the deep. He had to run over 25 metres before doing an amazing
overhead leap to catch Sylvester Clarke off Bruce Yardley.

Trailing the Windies by 117 runs in the first inning, Australia needed
373 to win against a fearsome attack of Michael Holding, Joel Garner,
Colin Croft and Clarke. Opening the second innings, Dyson dropped
anchor with Australia precariously perched on 4 for 169. Ultimately
he got in his nineties.

A quiet, elderly gentleman sitting on my left in the M.A. Noble Stand in the Sydney Cricket Ground suddenly started behaving oddly. He became pink in the face, stood up and sat down repeatedly and impatiently, started perspiring visibly and breathing heavily, clenching and unclenching his fist, and I thought he was having a heart attack. On being asked whether he was all right, he replied: 'That's my son, John, and he is about to hit a century in his very first Test against the Windies! I didn't see his century in the Leeds Test against the Poms last year, but hope he scores one today. But why is he taking ages? C'mon son!'

John looked cool in the middle but Dyson Senior and I died a thousand deaths as we bellowed 'Hit…Steady…Run…Don't run' till he got his ton, and the two of us did a Caribbean 'High Five'.

Australia drew the Test, thanks to Dyso's defence (127 runs in 377 minutes with 11 fours), but somehow after his century, everything seemed an anticlimax.

To go down memory lane, it was a prolonged ninety which got me hooked on cricket. The thrill of bicycling rather than an interest in the game prompted me, an 11-year-old country boy in India, to visit a stranger's house miles away to listen to my first cricket commentary.

An unofficial Test match was being played in Calcutta between a star-studded Commonwealth XI and India in December 1949. However, in our tiny village Udvada (180 kilometres from Bombay), electricity was available only from 7 to 11 p.m. and transistors were unheard of. The only battery-operated radio was owned by a cricket fanatic in the nearby village.

At that time cricket left me cold but the prospect of a long bicycle ride was exciting. When I reached the destination, there were some 15 listeners already tuned to the broadcast. I joined them and soon an expectant silence developed.

India's captain, Vijay Hazare, who is remembered in Australia for his twin hundreds in the Adelaide Test of 1948 against Ray Lindwall and Keith Miller, hit three fours in an over to reach 97. Had he reached his century in the next few minutes, my interest in cricket would have remained lukewarm, but Hazare took his time. It was gripping. My heart must have missed a beat several times as he struggled towards his ton. After 20 minutes, Hazare was still on 97. The radio room became crammed with people who kept asking: 'Has he got his hundred yet?'

Five more agonising minutes and he reached his century and then galloped to 175 not out. A cricket addict was born. Not because Hazare scored 175, but because he got stuck on 97 for so long.

At least this story had a happy ending. Not the wistful tale of boy Cowdrey. Colin Cowdrey, who went on to score 107 first-class centuries (including 22 in 114 Tests for England) played his first cricket match in 1940 when seven. In an Under-11 game for Homefield School in Surrey he saw the ball well and soon started timing it sweetly, despatching fours everywhere. After a couple of hours, there were cheers on the boundary line, the boys chanting: 'Seven more for your century, Colin'.

Colin carefully scored those seven runs and raised his bat with the panache of a youthful Denis Compton amid a standing ovation from his mates. Delighted, he threw away his wicket 'racing down the wicket to let myself be stumped by a third of the pitch and running on to the applauding welcoming committee on the boundary', he recalled in *MCC: The Autobiography of a Cricketer*. 'I had never been happier in my life.'

Nor was he so downcast as when told a few minutes later that, on recounting, his score was 93 and not 100. No wonder he had tears streaming down his chubby cheeks. News of this non-nervous ninety impressed his cricket-mad headmaster Charles Walford so much that he wrote to Jack Hobbs about this near miss. Three weeks later Master Cowdrey received an inspiring letter from the great man—accompanied by an autographed bat.

As a sequel, I am compelled to mention another ninety by Cowdrey in The Oval Test of 1964 against Australia 24 years later. He was on 93 (yes, again!) when rain washed out play—probably the only instance of weather preventing a batsman in the nineties reaching a Test century!

Dudley Nourse, the prolific South African batsman, remembered his first Test ninety many years after retiring from cricket. It happened in the Durban Test of December 1935. 'I was 91 and in sight of my first Test century against the Australians when [Bill] O'Reilly came back and posted two short legs, his suicide trap,' he wrote in his autobiography, *Cricket in the Blood*.

When Australian fielder Jack Fingleton showed reluctance to put 'his neck on the chop', the no-nonsense O'Reilly told him sternly to 'stay there and take your catches'. Soon Nourse played a fraction too soon and Fingleton caught him for 91.

'Here was a chance to be asked to plant a tree at Kingsmead and I got so near to an honour reserved for centurions in Test matches and bowlers who achieved exceptional figures,' lamented Nourse.

The next Test at Johannesburg which started on Christmas eve was equally traumatic for him. He made a duck in the first innings and was 96 in the second with 20 minutes of play still remaining. He desperately wanted to get those four runs by stumps to get it over and done with.

Just then, master spinners O'Reilly and Clarrie Grimmett held a mid-wicket conference with skipper Vic Richardson. Using a slightly altered field placement, the spin legends bowled an impeccable length and a tentative Nourse—with the Durban dismissal fresh in memory—could not add a run that day.

'That night I was abed early but with the thoughts of what might happen in the first or second over of a new day while I was accustoming myself afresh to conditions...I heard every hour strike till three o'clock in the morning when finally I went to sleep. The feeling of frustration was infuriating. The mortifying part was that I could do nothing about it.'

This anxiety proved unnecessary. The next morning Nourse not only got his 100 but went on to amass 231, then the highest score by a South African in a Test.

Sydney all-rounder Arthur Chipperfield thought he was lucky to be picked for the tour of England in 1934 after playing only three first-class games. Then came his Test debut at Trent Bridge, Nottingham and he wondered whether he was lucky at all. He frequently lofted the ball and reached 99 at lunch on the second day. So nervous was he, he could not touch food. To make matters worse, all around him were unsparing in giving advice till he became a nervous wreck.

To quote Frank Tyson in *The Century Makers*: 'That lunch must have been a meal of stomach-knotting tension for him, rendered completely indigestible by his falling to the first ball after the interval!' According to the official score-card, however, 'Chippers' was caught behind by Leslie Ames off Ken Farnes' third (and not first) delivery after lunch. 'I wish I had not caught it but had to,' commented Ames.

Cheerless Chippers became the first batsman and so far the only Australian to make 99 on his Test debut. He still remains the only one to score 99 in his first ever Test innings.

When the next Ashes Test was played at Trent Bridge in 1938, England's attacking batsman Charlie Barnett was on 98 at lunch on the opening day—perhaps thinking of Chipperfield's 'fatal' break. Happily, Barnett reached his century off the first ball after lunch with

A horror lunch break for the gloveless, luckless Arthur Chipperfield. On 99 at lunch in his Test debut, he was caught behind in the first over after lunch for 99. (Jack Pollard collection)

Steve Waugh was dismissed in his nineties in two successive Tests in 1988. In England the next year he scored two consecutive centuries followed by a 92. (*The Sydney Morning Herald*)

a four past extra cover. His only remorse was that he did not reach his hundred before lunch on the opening day; a rare feat achieved only by

Back to basics. Indian all-rounder Rusi Surti gave two chances when 99
in the Auckland Test of 1968. He was out in the next over for 99.
(Courtesy Rusi Surti)

Australia's Victor Trumper, Charlie Macartney and Don Bradman
before him and Pakistan's Majid Khan after him.

Apart from Chippers, the only other batsman to tumble on 99
on Test debut was the bespectacled West Indian Bob Christiani.
He looked surprised when given out lbw for 99 by a home umpire
in the second innings of the Bridgetown Test against England in
1948.

By coincidence, the only two batsmen to be dismissed for 99 in their Test bow had names starting with Ch. The two Ch's of Test cricket, however, had the consolation of recording a Test century later on.

Not for Rusi Surti, the left-handed Indian all-rounder, such consolation. In the Auckland Test against New Zealand in 1968, Surti played with supreme confidence and was a delight to watch as he approached his maiden Test century. But soon he suffered the 99-butterfly syndrome. At that score he was dropped by Mark Burgess in the slips off Garry Bartlett and in the next over Graham Dowling grassed him at square-leg off Bruce Taylor. Still not chastened, he nicked again and was snapped up by Burgess in the slips off Bartlett. For 99! Nervous 99 in excelsis!

Surti played two more Tests but failed to score a century. Later, he became the first Indian to play Sheffield Shield (for Queensland in the 1970s), hit a hundred and was the first to perform a hat-trick for Queensland. Now settled in Brisbane, he recalls the Auckland Test with mixed feelings:

'I was more anxious than nervous to get my maiden Test century. All I wanted was to nick a single to achieve what I had never attained before—and as it turned out—afterwards. I still remember returning to the pavilion a broken man, when a spectator walked towards me, put his hand over my shoulder, congratulated me and said, "I have watched cricket for 26 years and you're the first batsman I've seen dismissed for 99".'

2 Many Splendoured Nineties

At best, a ninety is a bronze medal;
at worst, a heart-wrenching experience.

What is more diabolical—to get a golden duck in successive Test innings (ask David Boon), to get four consecutive Test zeroes (ask Mark Waugh), or to be dismissed a few runs short of the coveted three figures (ask Boon, Slater, the Waughs or the other 272 out-in-the-nineties victims).

It's a moot point. A few ducks can put you out of a team, and if it happens to be a Test side, it means loss of earnings. It also results in lack of confidence and, in some cases, loss of face.

A ninety, on the other hand, keeps your selection guaranteed but on a personal note you perhaps suffer more. You have worked at your innings for hours, nurtured it with tender loving care, tamed all bowlers—fast and curvy—and are about to reap the harvest. A century, no less!

Then a loud appeal, umpire's raised finger and you retreat to the pavilion in a daze, a few runs short of a cherished dream. Complete silence apart from the occasional 'Bad luck, mate' from colleagues and opponents, and you hum the Kingston Trio's 'Hang down your head, Tom Dooley' in the shower.

However, Geoff Boycott was different. In the Port-of-Spain Test against the West Indies in 1974, he scored 99 and 112, the only batsman to make a 99 and a century in the same Test. Surprisingly, he was pleased with his 99 but was unhappy with his 112. The explanation, as given in *Boycott: The Autobiography* is typical of the man.

Boycott's batting (211 runs in the Test) and Tony Greig's bowling (13 for 156) had enabled England to win the Test by 25 runs and draw the series one-all. Had England lost the Test (and with it the series 0–2), there was no way Mike Denness, Boycott's arch rival for English captaincy, would have retained the leadership.

Wrote Boycott: 'the achievement [of scoring 112 in the second innings] was bitter-sweet and I would be a hypocrite not to admit that I was torn by it at the end'.

Denness accepted the congratulations for the Test win and retained the captaincy which could have gone to Boycott had England lost. At least that's how Boycott saw it. 'In simple terms, I had cost myself the captaincy of England,' he wrote. 'It would have been the easiest thing in the world to have given my wicket away in the second innings, especially after a big score in the first, and history would probably have turned out very differently.'

For England or for Boycott, one wonders.

Allan Border, with 27 Test centuries under his belt, went through 36 Tests and 49 months (from September 1988 to September 1992)

Another ninety? No worries. To Allan Border, his team came before personal glory. (Ken Piesse library)

without scoring a Test hundred. In the Adelaide Test against India in January 1992 he came very close to a hundred but put his country above self.

With the final over to go before tea break on the fourth day, Border on 90 told his partner Mike Whitney: 'We've got this over and then I'm declaring'.

A shocked Whitney pleaded: 'Why not get your century first, get the monkey off your back, AB, and then declare? Why not be selfish for once, mate?'

But Border was firm. He got a single off the first ball from Venkatapathy Raju to go to 91. Number 11 bat Whitney was seeing the ball well having added 42 for the last wicket. Desperately trying to give the strike to Border, Whitney slogged the ball to mid-on and was caught with Border remaining 91 not out.

'Team-mates and media blamed me for "tonking" the ball and robbing AB of a century,' Whitney said. 'Had he not made up his mind to declare, I would have defended and Border could have reached

Two faces of Michael Slater during the 1993 Perth Test. A glorious cover drive took him to his 90 (left). Soon he was caught behind for 99. 'I put my hand on the head in sheer disbelief,' Slater wrote. (*The Sydney Morning Herald*)

his ton after tea. All the same, AB's declaration was well-timed and we won in the final hour after a heroic fight-back by the Indians.'

Attacking New South Wales opening batsman Michael Slater scored a magnificent century in his second Test, against England at Lord's in 1993. 'It was an emotional moment for me to get a hundred at Lord's, especially being my first. With all the history at the ground and to do it on the hallowed turf, I was pretty out of control,' he recalled. And out of control he certainly was, waving his bat in the air like an Olympic fencing champion, kissing his helmet and punching the air à la Greg Matthews.

However, in the Perth Test against New Zealand five months later, it was a morose Slater who returned to the pavilion caught behind off Dipak Patel for 99. Patel instinctively knew what went through his victim's mind as he himself had fallen at 99 against England at Christchurch the previous year.

Slater was stunned. He staggered in disappointment, stood clasping his helmet for painful seconds and desolately left the ground.

To quote Slater: 'I put my hand on the head in sheer disbelief. Dipak had not turned the ball all day. When he bowled one down leg-side with me on 99, I thought I would poke it for a single to get my hundred. To my horror, I gloved it and was caught behind. I was shattered to go so close and miss out.'

Slater returned to his sizzling form in the next Test at Hobart with a career-best 168, but was lucky to escape being run-out when 99. Had he been declared out at that score he would have become the first man out for 99 in consecutive Test innings. 'Nervousness made me go for that unlikely single,' Slater commented later.

His obsession with nineties continued in the Sydney Test against South Africa in January 1994. He top-scored in this thrilling match by making 92, describing this innings as 'the hardest day of Test cricket I have played and I learnt a lot.'

Four Tests and 12 weeks later, he was given out lbw for 95 in the Durban Test. Thus in 126 days (from 15 November 1993 to 21 March 1994), Slater was dismissed in his nineties three times—almost once every month. Had he been adjudged run-out in the Hobart Test for 99, Slater would have had a rare sequence of 99, 99, 28, 32 and 92 in consecutive Test innings; closest to Australian great Clem Hill's 99, 98 and 97 in successive Test knocks in 1902.

This is how left-handed Hill's sequence of bad luck started. In the exciting Melbourne Test starting in the New Year of 1902, Australia was bowled out for 112 on a treacherous pitch but obtained a lead of 41 runs and went on to win the Test by 229 runs. Batting at number 7 in the second innings on a pitch improving by the hour, Hill eventually fell to Sydney F. Barnes (who claimed 13 for 163) at 99. Hill was the first batsman to make 99 in a Test.

The next Test at Adelaide brought further heartache for Hill. He scored 98 and 97, described by English writer Simon R. Wilde as 'an unparalleled spell of nonagenarian's neurosis.'

As Hill walked off after being caught for 98 in the first innings, English fielder J.T. Tyldesley urged him to return to the crease, saying: 'Go back, Clem, I took the catch standing on the bicycle track.' But Hill kept walking, explaining that the captains had agreed that the fence was the boundary and not the bicycle track. Under today's rules this would be considered a six and Hill would have got his century.

His bad luck continued to hound him in the second innings. He chopped down a ball when just three runs short of his century and to his horror saw it rolling back towards the stumps. He swung around to stop the perfect 'stump-landing' but knocked off the leg bail with his bat instead.

When luck is down, freak happenings are not far away.

Despite such mishaps, Hill topped 500 runs in the series, becoming the first batsman to do so without hitting a century. That year he went on to make 1000 Test runs in a calendar year, the first player to do so. England's Denis Compton was the next one to achieve it, 45 years later in 1947.

South Africa's opening batsman, Andrew Hudson, must be excused for feeling a bit jinxed. At the time of going to press, it seems that every time he scores a ninety or a century, his country loses. In his Test debut in April 1992, he amassed 163 against the West Indies at Bridgetown—the first South African ever to hit a ton on debut—and his team lost. He made a patient 90 in the Adelaide Test in early 1994 and South Africa lost. Then in the Cape Town Test, also against Australia in March 1994, he scored 102 and his country lost again!

We can imagine—tongue in cheek of course—his captain imploring Hudson to throw his wicket away when in the eighties and the opponents trying their hardest to donate easy runs!

3 Colour Them Indefatigable

Those who swim oceans often get drowned near the coast.
—An old Indian proverb

Bob Simpson is a typical Aussie battler who takes things as they come; no fuss, no emotional outbursts and very few quotable quotes. Yet when he scored a century in the Old Trafford (Manchester) Test of 1964, he was besides himself with joy. He exclaimed: 'You beaut, I've got it at last. Thank God that's over. I can now get on with making some runs.'

He certainly got going, making 311 runs in 762 minutes, still the highest score in an Old Trafford Test and the highest by an Australian captain. Only Don Bradman had amassed a higher score for Australia; 334 against England at Leeds in 1930, before he was captain.

It was not so much the triple century which delighted Simmo as the magic three figures, the 100 against his name which had eluded him for so long.

Simpson had made his Test debut seven years earlier in 1957 and had played 51 Test innings without making a Test hundred. He had come close on three occasions: 92 in the tied Test against the West Indies at Brisbane in 1960–61, another 92 at Melbourne in the same series and 91 v. England at Sydney in 1962–63. On all three occasions he was bowled by off-spinners—Sonny Ramadhin, Lance Gibbs and Fred Titmus.

When he reached 90 in that Old Trafford Test, he was under intense pressure. He remembered in *Captain's Story*: 'Whereas there were gaps in the field when I was still in the eighties, suddenly there seemed to be none. Eventually I was within one stroke of that unattainable goal.'

An unhappy Bob Simpson is adjudged out and Bill Lawry looks on grimly. Simmo made three nineties before his first Test century, a triple ton at Old Trafford in 1964. (*The Sydney Morning Herald*)

He turned the next ball to fine leg. Memories of his three previous nineties floated in his mind. Surely someone will catch it or throw it back to run him out, he feared. But lo, the ball was on its way and at long last he had got his century.

'Nobody can describe the feeling of relief that flooded through me when that magical three-digit number went up on the scoreboard and the crowd burst into applause,' he reminisced. 'I don't know of any player who was on the international scene as long as I without scoring a century. I had been in the nineties [in Tests] so many times and failed to make it. I was feeling a bit silly about it by this stage. Here I was, an Australian batsman for years, I had scored about forty centuries in first-class cricket, I had many 200s in the scorebook and a 300—yet I had not scored a Test century. The trouble was purely psychological, it had become a tremendous mental block.'

The Old Trafford triple ton removed his frustrating mental block for sure and he went on to hit nine more Test hundreds and only an additional 90.

Simpson's contemporary Ian Redpath started his Test career with a 97 against South Africa at Melbourne in 1963–64 but had to wait till his 49th Test innings for his maiden hundred which came against the Windies at Sydney in 1968–69.

In many ways, the only thing worse than to be out in the nineties is to be left not out in the nineties, when number 11 bat holes out and you are left high and dry, sighing: 'Where's the justice? I did everything right.'

South Africa's 'Grand Old Man', A.W. 'Dave' Nourse (father of Dudley) had to suffer this exasperation twice. The first time was in his maiden Test against England at Johannesburg in 1905–06 when he scored an unbeaten 93 and steered his country to a memorable first win over England. He added 48 runs for the tenth wicket with his captain Percy Sherwell for a thrilling one-wicket triumph.

Six years later Dave Nourse ran out of partners when making 92 not out against Australia in Melbourne in 1911 as South Africa lost by a huge margin of 530 runs. His first Test hundred (111) finally came in November 1921, at Johannesburg against Australia, 20 years after his Test debut. He was 43, which made him the oldest cricketer to make his first and only Test hundred.

The inimitable Garry Sobers had to wait for five years and 29 Test innings to hit his maiden Test century. And like Simpson's, it was also a triple ton, 365 not out, which remained the highest score in Test cricket till eclipsed by Brian Lara's magnificent 375 in 1994. In the Kingston Test against Pakistan in 1958 Sobers added 446 runs for the second wicket with Conrad Hunte. However, unlike Simpson, Sobers had not scored any ninety before his triple joy. He made up for that 'lapse' by making five nineties (once not out) subsequently, and also 25 more Test hundreds.

Rodney Marsh, the beefy Australian wicket-keeper (whose 355 dismissals behind the stumps in 96 Tests is a record) also made four nineties and three centuries. He remembers his first ninety, an unbeaten 92 against England at Melbourne during his maiden Test series in 1970–71. To quote from his autobiographical *You'll Keep*:

'Later in the Australian innings [Bill] Lawry brought the wrath of the world down on his shoulders in an incident involving me. Even his own partisan Melbourne crowd couldn't remain faithful to him after he declared with my score only eight runs short of a century, which would have been the first by an Australian keeper in a Test match. I wasn't at all upset about it…I had expected Bill to declare long before, so I guess I was lucky to have even reached the nineties'.

All the same, English all-rounder Basil D'Oliveira commented to Marsh: 'If I'd known he [Lawry] was going to pull out, I'd have given you a couple of full tosses to let you get your first "ton" '.

Rod Marsh registered two nineties before becoming the first Australian wicket-keeper to hit a Test century. (Ken Piesse library)

Later, Ian Chappell comforted Marsh: 'Let's face it, the team comes first, doesn't it?'

Marsh had the mortification of making one more ninety before becoming the first Australian wicket-keeper to register a Test ton: 118 against Pakistan at Adelaide in 1972–73.

The fluent backfoot strokeplayer Steve Waugh had to wait for four years and 26 Tests to break the century barrier. His timing had marked him as a batsman of the future after his Test debut as a 20-year-old against India in 1985–86. But though he scored well, including two consecutive 90s against the West Indies at Brisbane and Perth in 1988–89, a Test century had eluded him. He decisively made up for it at Headingley, Leeds, against England in 1989 with a dazzling 177 not out in 242 balls (24 fours), and in the second Test at Lord's with a mature, unbeaten 152. To quote *Wisden 1990*: 'In more than a century of Tests, there cannot have been many better maiden hundreds than Waugh's at Headingley'.

Bespectacled New South Wales batsman Dirk Wellham will never forget his Test debut. Against England in the final Test at The Oval in 1981, he stayed on 99 for 27 harrowing minutes. The power of one, the final hurdle, appeared to be too much for the Test tyro, as he played and missed several times and offered a catch to Geoff Boycott at mid-off.

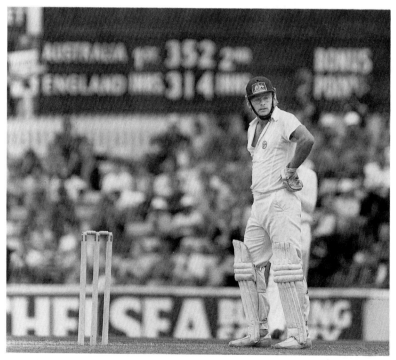

Dirk Wellham stayed on 99 for 27 harrowing minutes in his Test debut at The Oval in 1981. (Patrick Eagar)

He had almost started to walk back when 'to my shock and relief Boycott dropped it', recalled Wellham, smiling through his glasses. He went on to score 103 in 266 minutes with 12 fours, and was 'rewarded' by the selectors by being dropped in the next Test. Dirk the 'smirk' forced his way back into the Australian team, played five more Tests but without recapturing his Oval touch.

Wellham, the only Australian to score both a first-class and Test century on debut, revealed the anguish of his frenetic wait on 99 to the Melbourne branch of the Australian Cricket Society:

'I had raced from the 60s to the 90s as the word came out that we were going to push it along for a declaration on the fourth afternoon of the Test. But the combination of a player in his first Test about to score a century and the appearance of a thick, dark cloud over the ground caused our captain Kim Hughes to send a message that I could take my time.

'After I had been on 99 for fifteen minutes, the drinks break came and brought some relief from the seemingly endless tension. I drank, chatted about nothing and returned to pick up my bat and began to pull on the gloves. As I composed myself to continue, a voice from nearby said "You've done all the hard work, don't throw it away now".

'It was Ian Botham, the man who had been striving to get me out. Ten minutes after the resumption, my instincts took over and I punched a shortish delivery through to the cover boundary. It was hard to believe I had scored a century in my first Test. It was *Boy's Own* stuff and I didn't know what to do or where to look.'

Subsequently, Wellham created a unique record by captaining three States—New South Wales, Tasmania and Queensland—in the Sheffield Shield. When representing Tasmania in Shield cricket, he made six nineties in three seasons without once reaching 100:

1988–89	92	v. Queensland, Brisbane
	90*	v. Western Australia, Perth
	94	v. South Australia, Adelaide
1989–90	90	v. New South Wales, Hobart
	91	v. New South Wales, Sydney
1990–91	95	v. Victoria, Hobart

* = not out

In the limited-overs internationals, Wellham's top score was 97 which came against England at Sydney on 22 January 1987. Now retired, his wait for a century in a limited-overs international has gone unfulfilled. However, Wellham's crawl to his debut century in The Oval Test in 1981 is still remembered by his mother, Mrs Nancy Wellham. Watching the Test on TV from Sydney, she had remarked: 'It seemed as if he almost became paralysed, but apparently Ian Botham gave him a word of encouragement...I was worried Boycott may have dropped that catch on 99 on purpose, but they said, "Oh, no, Boycott would't do that".'

Patience Award at Test level should go to the South African all-rounder Trevor Goddard. He amassed 2077 runs including three nineties—90, 99 and 93—before making his first and only Test hundred which came in his 62nd Test innings: 112 v. England at Johannesburg in 1964–65. Colour him, and others in this chapter, indefatigable.

4 The Test 99ers

> If Ivan Lendl was a cricketer, he would score
> 99 every time at Lord's.

A century is to be savoured and cherished. Yet a 99 is wistfully remembered longer as it depicts both achievement and failure simultaneously, when near enough is not good enough but a touch more dramatic.

Forty-six batsmen have scored 99 runs on 50 occasions in 118 years of Test cricket, with Clem Hill, as stated earlier, being the pioneer in January 1902. Three of these 46 members have been dismissed *twice* for 99 in Test cricket: Mike J.K. Smith of England, West Indian Richie Richardson and John Wright of New Zealand. Geoff Boycott is unique. He was dismissed for a 99 once and remained 99 not out in another Test—carrying his bat. (See footnote, page 45.)

Boycott is also the only batsman to score a 99 and a century in the same Test (v. West Indies at Port-of-Spain in 1974.) Also, he is one of three batsmen after India's Pankaj Roy and Pakistan's Mushtaq Mohammad to register a duck and a 99 in the same Test. As stated before, Australia's Arthur Chipperfield and West Indian Bob Christiani made 99 on Test debut, and Bruce Mitchell (South Africa) is the only one to do so in his final Test appearance.

As at 1 June 1994, batsmen scoring 99 runs in a Test innings are listed below:

Batsman	Opponent	Venue	Series
Australia (14 batsmen 14 times)			
C. Hill	England	Melbourne	1901–02
C.G. Macartney	England	Lord's	1912
A.G. Chipperfield	England	Nottingham	1934
W.A. Brown	India	Melbourne	1947–48

Batsman	Opponent	Venue	Series
K.R. Miller	England	Adelaide	1950–51
A.R. Morris	S. Africa	Melbourne	1952–53
C.C. McDonald	S. Africa	Cape Town	1957–58
R.M. Cowper	England	Melbourne	1965–66
I.M. Chappell	India	Calcutta	1969–70
R. Edwards	England	Lord's	1975
K.J. Hughes	England	Perth	1979–80
D.M. Jones	New Zealand	Perth	1989–90
M.E. Waugh	England	Lord's	1993
M.J. Slater	New Zealand	Perth	1993–94

England (10 batsmen 12 times)

H. Sutcliffe	S. Africa	Cape Town	1927–28
E. Paynter	Australia	Lord's	1938
N.W.D. Yardley	S. Africa	Nottingham	1947
M.J.K. Smith	S. Africa	Lord's	1960
M.J.K. Smith	Pakistan	Lahore	1961–62
E.R. Dexter	Australia	Brisbane	1962–63
D.L. Amiss	Pakistan	Karachi	1972–73
G. Boycott	West Indies	Port-of-Spain	1973–74
G. Boycott[a]	Australia	Perth	1979–80
G.A. Gooch	Australia	Melbourne	1979–80
M.D. Moxon	New Zealand	Auckland	1987–88
M.A. Atherton	Australia	Lord's	1993

South Africa (3 batsmen 3 times)

G.A. Faulkner	England	Cape Town	1909-10
B. Mitchell	England	Port Elizabeth	1948-49
T.L. Goddard	England	The Oval	1960

West Indies (5 batsmen 6 times)

R.J. Christiani	England	Bridgetown	1947–48
A.F. Rae	New Zealand	Auckland	1951–52
R.B. Kanhai	India	Madras	1958–59
M.L.C. Foster	India	Port-of-Spain	1970–71
R.B. Richardson	India	Port-of-Spain	1988–89
R.B. Richardson	Australia	Bridgetown	1990–91

New Zealand (4 batsmen 5 times)

J.E.F. Beck	S. Africa	Cape Town	1953–54
R.J. Hadlee	England	Christchurch	1983–84
J.G. Wright	Australia	Melbourne	1987–88
J.G. Wright	England	Christchurch	1991–92
D.N. Patel	England	Christchurch	1991–92

Agony for falling twice for 99 shows on Kiwi John Wright's face. (Ken Piesse library)

A devastated Graham Gooch returns to the pavilion, run out for 99, just before tea in the Melbourne Test of 1979–80. (Ken Piesse library)

Richie Richardson pulls in crowds with his pull shots. He is one of a small handful of batsmen to be dismissed twice for 99 in Test cricket. (Ken Piesse library)

Batsman	Opponent	Venue	Series
India (5 batsmen five times)			
Pankaj Roy	Australia	Delhi	1959–60
M.L. Jaisimha	Pakistan	Kanpur	1960–61
A.L. Wadekar	Australia	Melbourne	1967–68
R.F. Surti	New Zealand	Auckland	1967–68
N.S. Sidhu	Sri Lanka	Bangalore	1993–94
Pakistan (5 batsmen 5 times)			
Maqsood Ahmed	India	Lahore	1954–55
Majid Khan	England	Karachi	1972–73
Mushtaq Mohammad	England	Karachi	1972–73
Javed Miandad	India	Bangalore	1983–84
Salim Malik	England	Leeds	1987

Sri Lanka (none)

Zimbabwe (none)

[a] Boycott scored 99 not out, carrying his bat

Aggressive Indian opener Navjot Sidhu is a recent member of the 99 Club. (Ken Piesse library)

Country-wise break-up for Test 99ers is presented below:

Country	Batsmen	Instances
Australia	14	14
England	10	12[a]
South Africa	3	3
West Indies	5	6
New Zealand	4	5
India	5	5
Pakistan	5	5
Sri Lanka	0	0
Zimbabwe	0	0
Total	46	50

[a] Boycott's unbeaten 99 in Perth 1979-80 is included

Of the 49 dismissals for 99 in Test matches, almost half (24) were caught, 10 run out, 7 bowled, 6 out leg-before-wicket and 2 stumped.

Australian spectators have witnessed most Test 99s, 13; followed by the English, 10; New Zealanders and Indians, 6 each; South Africans, West Indians and Pakistanis, 5 each. Newcomers to Test status, Sri Lankans and Zimbabweans have yet to see a 99 in a Test match.

The Melbourne Cricket Ground has 'hosted' the greatest number of 99s, 7—including the first ever by Clem Hill in 1902. Lord's has witnessed 6; Cape Town and Perth 4 each; Karachi, Port-of-Spain, Auckland and Christchurch 3 each; Nottingham, Lahore, Bridgetown and Bangalore 2 each; and Adelaide, Calcutta, Brisbane, Port Elizabeth, The Oval, Madras, Delhi, Kanpur and Leeds, one each.

All three 99s at Karachi came in the same match, Pakistan v. England in 1972–73. The unique '99 hat-trick' was achieved by Denis Amiss, Majid Khan and Mushtaq Mohammad. Amiss reached the nineties in each of the three Tests in the series, having hit hundreds in the previous two Tests at Lahore and Hyderabad.

Apart from Karachi, three Test grounds have provided multiple 99ers; Perth (Kim Hughes and Geoff Boycott in 1979–80 in the match remembered for Dennis Lillee's aluminium bat episode), Christchurch (John Wright and Dipak Patel in 1991–92) and Lord's (Mark Waugh and Michael Atherton in 1993). Interestingly, England was involved in all four of these series.

Three batsmen finished the 1979–80 Test series between Australia and England with a top score of 99: Graham Gooch 99 run out, Geoff Boycott 99 not out and Kim Hughes 99. David Gower narrowly missed out, remaining unbeaten on 98 at Sydney. Greg Chappell also scored an undefeated 98 in the Sydney Test but his highest score in that series was 114 (at Melbourne).

Post World War II batsmen Bill Brown, Arthur Morris, John Beck, Rohan Kanhai, M.L. Jaisimha, Mike Smith (at Lahore), Mushtaq Mohammad, Gooch, Patel and Atherton had the additional misfortune to be run out for 99. Gooch ran himself out in the final over before tea going for the single which would have given him his maiden Test century. He later went on to hit 19 centuries at Test level (as at 1 June 1994), including 333 and 123 in the same Test against India at Lord's in 1990. M.L. Jaisimha of India batted for 504 minutes for his 99, when he finally ran himself out, in December 1960. This is the longest any batsman has taken for his ninety.

Some 99ers never registered a Test ton. Rusi Surti, as mentioned earlier, was dropped *twice* on 99 and was caught without adding a run. As with Norman Yardley, Beck, Maqsood Ahmed, Martyn Moxon and Patel, 99 was to be Surti's highest score.

The above Unlucky Six must be regretting turning down a single somewhere in the course of their innings. Moxon was particularly unfortunate. In the Auckland Test of 1988, a sweetly timed sweep by him was signalled as 3 leg byes when he was on 32. So, morally, Moxon deserved a century. To quote David Frith from *Wisden Cricket Monthly*: 'The only comfort one could offer was that Moxon will probably be remembered more for 99, than if he had scored 102.'

For 30 years (from 1953 to 1983) John Beck had the dubious distinction of being the only member of the 99 Club for New Zealand. In his second Test at Cape Town, he was a teenager when run out for 99. It was a remarkable four week period for him. He was selected for the 1953–54 tour of South Africa without having played a single first-class match. He started off poorly, his first three innings on the tour yielding 5, 0 and 0. In the second Test at Johannesburg, he made 16 and 7 on a 'lethal pitch'—to quote New Zealand columnist Nigel Smith.

In the third Test at Cape Town, the visitors were well-placed at 4 for 271 when Beck joined John Reid. They added 174 for the fifth wicket in 150 minutes. After Reid departed for 135, Beck started attacking. At the non-striker's end, he responded to a call for a quick single by Eric Dempster but was run out by a direct hit from Dick Westcott.

Oddly, Beck was not aware that he was on 99 then. Only on his return to the dressing room when the genial Bert Sutcliffe put his arm round his shoulder to console him did the reality dawn on him. He played six more Tests and was discarded at the age of 21 without being given a chance to hit a hundred.

Richard Hadlee was the second Kiwi to make a Test 99, against England at Christchurch in February 1984. As England was skittled out for 82 and 93, Hadlee's 99 off only 81 balls (in 111 minutes and embellished with 18 fours) looks huge in comparison. Unlike countrymen Beck before him and Dipak Patel after him (both run out for 99) Hadlee had the consolation of scoring two Test centuries later on.

The elegant Mark Waugh was going serenely towards his Test century in the Lord's Test of 1993. It was the anniversary of the Battle of Waterloo and it seemed everything was set up for him for a big score. The openers Mark Taylor and Michael Slater had hit centuries,

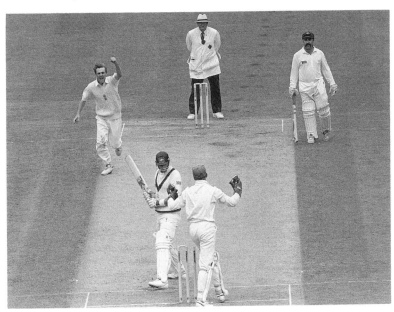

Mark Waugh bowled by Phil Tufnell for 99 at Lord's in 1993. David Boon, on 97 then, went on to compile an unbeaten 164. (Patrick Eager)

David Boon was in his 80s and 'Junior' Waugh on 99. Not only did Waugh need a single to reach his first Test hundred in England, but that hundred would also have established a unique record as Boon went on to score a ton. Never in Test history have the first four batsmen hit centuries in the one innings.

With Waugh on 99, everyone was waiting for history in the making. Hands were clasped together in anticipation of clapping, lungs filled in expectation of cheering and many hearts were in his supporters' mouths.

Leg-spinner Philip Tufnell delivered into the rough patch and bowled Waugh via his pad; a horrifying spectacle for his fans. Mark was too dazed to remove his helmet as he returned to the pavilion. This is how Steve Waugh describes his twin brother's dismissal in his *Ashes Diary*:

'When Mark reached 99, all the [Australian] players congregated on the balcony in preparation for a celebration. But, on this occasion, that preparation was tragically cut short. A Tufnell delivery cannoned off Junior's pads and clipped his off-stump, robbing him of every cricketer's dream—a century at Lord's.

'They say that twins have some form of ESP or that they are affected by events that happen to each other. Well, on that occasion, it felt as if *I* had been dismissed one short of 100, such was my disappointment. I'm sure Mark's disappointment would be magnified many more times over. That one delivery will surely be replayed in his mind a thousand times tonight [18 June 1993], and all the while he'll be hoping for time to turn back and give him another shot at history.'

Lord's was to witness another tragedy two days later. England, 427 runs behind, were fighting back in the second innings to save the Test and were 1 for 173, Atherton playing stylishly and with strong determination.

When 97, he placed an Allan Border delivery off his hip on the on side. It was racing towards the ropes which would bring up his 100. But Merv Hughes, the hirsute never-say-die character, chased the ball like a man possessed and picked it up inches from the rope. At precisely that time Atherton turned and headed off for the third run which would give him his century.

However, Mike Gatting spotted the danger and sent him back. Atherton slipped and fell on the ground, out of the crease. Hughes' return was brilliantly picked on the bounce by keeper Ian Healy and the stumps were broken, as was Atherton's spirit. 'If he had been on seven or 87, a third run would not have been contemplated,' wrote John Thicknesse in *Wisden 1994*. He called it 'a moment of masochistic madness.'

Cricket looked such a diabolical game then, even on TV thousands of kilometres away, as Atherton on his hands and knees tried desperately to crawl back to the crease.

His 'slipshod' dismissal for 99 inspired Paul Weston to write a poem in *Wisden Cricket Monthly* of August 1993:

> *Slipshod*
> A wanton dismissal, admittedly,
> But pity poor Atherton's lot,
> For what could be more ignominious
> Than a 'carpeting' there on the spot?
> The gentle reproaches of hindsight
> Will duly invite him to see
> The sorrow at hand for the footloose
> Who fervently fancy three!

The things some batsmen do to join the exclusive Test 99 Club! After all, over 2000 centuries have been recorded but only 50 99s.

Footnote In the Headingley (Leeds) Test against South Africa in August 1994, Michael Atherton became the fifth batsman after Mike Smith, Geoff Boycott, Richie Richardson and John Wright to register *two* Test 99s.

A majestic hook by Alvin Kallicharran. He holds the record of scoring most Test nineties, eight. (Ken Piesse library)

5 Ninety, Ninety on the Board

The 90 men are victims of thoughtless partners, ruthless skippers, rain, time, vandals, rioters, flukes, inept umpiring, amazing fielding, and occasionally …plain nerves, a bad shot or a good ball.

—Phill Cartwright

Australian Test cricketers have many firsts to their credit. In the inaugural Test match against England at Melbourne in March 1877, Australian opener Charles Bannerman scored the first century, skipper Dave Gregory won the first toss and his brother, Edward, made the first duck. Bill Midwinter became the first bowler to take five wickets in an innings while John Blackham effected the first stumping.

In Test number three, also at Melbourne, Fred 'Demon' Spofforth became the first bowler to take a hat-trick and capture 10 wickets in a Test (6 for 48 and 7 for 62).

Later, in the Sydney Test against England in 1883, Charles Bannerman's younger brother, Alec, scored 94 in 450 minutes, the first batsman to succumb to nervous nineties in Test annals. He followed it with a 91, also against England at Sydney in 1891. He remains first among six batsmen (the others being Australia's Tommy Andrews, West Indians Derek Sealy and Deryck Murray, India's Chetan Chauhan and England's Geoff Miller) to score two nineties but never a century at Test level. Chauhan is the only player to make 2000 Test runs (2084) without hitting a Test ton.

Allan Border is the only one to hit a ninety not out (98) and a 100 not out in the same Test (v. West Indies at Port-of-Spain in 1983–84). Border considers these two innings as among the best he has played. *Wisden 1985* wrote: 'Two epic innings by Border [in this Test] stood between Australia and defeat…He offered not a single chance although batting under great pressure.'

England's Paul Gibb was the first batsman to score a ninety (93) and a century (103) on debut (v. South Africa in Johannesburg in' 1938–39). Also, West Indies strokeplayer Gordon Greenidge started his Test career with a mixed bag of 93 run out and 107 against India at Bangalore in 1974. Although he registered 18 more Test hundreds, he is more remembered as the only batsman to record nineties in both innings of a Test on two occasions. The first time was when he made 91 and 96 against Pakistan at Georgetown in 1976–77 and later 91 and 97 against New Zealand at Christchurch in 1979–80.

Only Clem Hill (98 and 97 in Adelaide in 1902) and Frank Woolley (95 and 93 for England v. Australia at Lord's in 1921) have done it once each in Test annals. England's captain Ted Dexter scored 99 and 93 in successive Test innings but in different Tests against Australia, at Brisbane and Melbourne in 1962–63. Similarly, New Zealand's Jeremy Coney made 98 and 93 in successive innings v. Australia at Christchurch and Auckland in 1985–86, Steve Waugh 90 and 91 in successive Test innings v. West Indies at Brisbane and Perth in 1988–89 and David Boon 94 not out and 97 in consecutive innings v. England at Melbourne and Sydney in 1990–91.

Amay Khurasiya of Madhya Pradesh, India, is the only batsman to score 99 in both innings of a first-class match (99 and 99 not out at Nagpur in 1991–92). In another first-class match, India's B.B. Nimbalkar scored 99 and 95 in a Ranji Trophy match in 1947–48. He made up for these near misses by amassing 443 not out (50 fours and a six) the next season for Maharashtra v. Kathiawar at Pune—the fourth highest individual score in first-class cricket.

Harold Larwood's lightning speed as a bowler terrified many Australian batsmen and electrified home spectators during the controversial Bodyline series of 1932–33, and effectively reduced Bradman's batting average by half. Larwood, surprisingly, also shone in the final Test of the series at Sydney as a batsman. The Nottinghamshire coal miner, now happily settled in Sydney and almost blind, remembers his 98 in 135 minutes at Sydney with pride.

'I was sent in as a night watchman and started confidently the next morning. I did not realise I was near a "hoondred" [sic] till my partner Maurice Leyland told me to go easy as I was on 98. That made me tense and uncomfortable. The previous four balls I had hit for 2, 6, 2 and 4 with confidence. The next ball was an easy one but instead of

Gordon Greenidge started his Test career with 93 run out and 107. He is the only batsman to hit 90s in both innings of a Test twice. (Ken Piesse library)

Easy come, easy go. A century, a ninety or a duck came alike to David Gower. He enjoyed his batting and so did his fans. (Ken Piesse library)

hitting it with force, I checked my shot and skied it. And guess what? Bert Ironmonger, the worst catcher in the world, got under it and caught it. I was then very disappointed to miss my "hoondred", but in retrospect I'm pleased. Had I reached that century, it would have been forgotten soon. But because I missed it by two runs, that innings is talked about even now.'

The 1956 Ashes series in England is remembered for an odd reason. Not a single Australian scored a century in the five Tests; highest being 97 by Richie Benaud. Also, in the 1985–86 series, no Englishman could register a hundred against the West Indies, the best being David Gower's 90.

In the three-Test series between England and the Windies in 1966 in England, as many as six batsmen got out in their nineties; Colin Milburn 94 on debut, Tom Graveny 96, Jim Parks 91, Seymour Nurse 93, Colin Cowdrey 96 and Garry Sobers 94.

Another 'pandemic' of nineties occurred in 1973 when five batsmen were dismissed in their nineties in five days, from March 24 to 28: Ian Chappell (97) and Alvin Kallicharran (91) in the Port-of-Spain Test and Denis Amiss, Majid Khan and Mushtaq Mohammad (all for 99) in the 99-rich Karachi Test. The only time both the opening batsmen were dismissed in their nineties in Test cricket was when India's Sunil Gavaskar scored 97 and Chetan Chauhan 93 at Lahore against Pakistan in 1978–79.

The Christchurch Test between New Zealand and England of January 1992 was unique in that four batsmen were dismissed in their nineties—including two Kiwis for 99. Dipak Patel went for a third run but was run out, by a whisker, by Derek Pringle—not known for his strong arm. Patel's was an attacking innings—coming off only 134 balls with 11 fours and two sixes. When on 97, he pulled Chris Lewis to deep mid wicket and sensed the three for his maiden century. Pringle retrieved the ball, but with no throwing arm, was obliged to 'bowl' the ball back. Patel hesitated, then took off for the third run but Pringle surprised him by his accuracy.

Patel said afterwards: 'I was pretty dumbstruck. I didn't know how to react in the dressing room. But people put me right. They said, "although it was 99 you know yourself it was worth a 100". I looked at it that way and always will.'

In the second innings, another New Zealander, John Wright, succumbed to a tragic error of judgment when he was steering his country to the safety of a draw on the final day. He was tied down on

Keith Miller, the dashing cavalier, is bowled by Johnny Wardle for 109
in the 1953 Lord's Test. Another spinner, Doug Wright, had bowled him
for 99 in the Adelaide Test of 1950–51. (Ken Piesse library)

Ian Chappell on a hooking spree. He scored four Test nineties which
included a 99 at Calcutta in 1969. (Ken Piesse library)

99 for 23 minutes either side of the tea interval, got impatient at Philip Tufnell's accuracy and for the first time in more than six hours went down the pitch to try to hit him over the top. He missed but survived. He charged again, was stranded by a wider ball bouncing out of the footmarks and was stumped. He became the second batsman, after Pakistan's Maqsood Ahmed in 1954–55, to be stumped for 99.

Two Englishmen, Robin Smith (96 with 16 fours) and Alan Lamb (93 with 13 fours and a six) also fell short of their hundreds in this Test won by England by an innings.

West Indies all-rounder Keith Boyce showed true-grit in the Adelaide Test against Australia in 1975–76. He was 65 when joined by last man Lance Gibbs. Boyce took his score to 95 in a 35-run partnership at stumps, but the next morning Gibbs was bowled for 3. Boyce's unbeaten 95 in 140 minutes enabled the Windies to avoid the follow-on but not to save the Test.

Two batsmen—both elegant and prolific—scored an identical number of runs in each innings of a Test. They were England's David Gower and Australia's Greg Chappell who scored 3 in the first innings and 98 not out in the second during the Sydney Test of January 1980. Lack of support left Gower two short of a ton while Australia's six-wicket win robbed Chappell of his century. Chappell was on strike on 94 with Australia needing only one run to win. Ian Botham, in a rare generous mood, deliberately bowled a long hop to give Chappell an opportunity to reach his hundred with a six. Chappell hooked hard and high but could manage only a four.

As at 1 June 1994, 276 batsmen have recorded 485 nineties in 1260 Tests. (For details, see Appendix.) Alvin Kallicharran from the West Indies has made most nineties in Test history, eight in 66 Tests, once remaining unbeaten on 92.

Another eight batsmen have scored nineties in five or more Test innings; Clem Hill (Australia), Rohan Kanhai (West Indies), Geoff Boycott (England) and Gordon Greenidge (West Indies) six each; and Ken Barrington (England), Garry Sobers (West Indies), Sunil Gavaskar (India) and David Boon (Australia), five each.

Who have been the bowlers men fear most when in the ninties? Well, India's Kapil Dev has dismissed most such batsmen, nine, followed by Richard Hadlee and Malcolm Marshall (West Indies), six each and Lance Gibbs (West Indies), Bruce Yardley (Australia), Derek Underwood (England) and Ian Botham (England), five each.

The Melbourne Cricket Ground has witnessed most Test nineties, 37; Lord's is only a whisker away, 35; then the Sydney Cricket Ground and The Oval, 28 each; Adelaide Oval, 26; Port-of-Spain, 25 and Johannesburg and Leeds, 22 each.

Of the 437 times batsmen have been dismissed in their nineties, a majority were caught, 262 (59.95%), 242 in the field or by the wicket-keeper and 20 by the bowler; 86 (19.68%) bowled; 52 (11.90%) were lbw victims; 22 (5.03%) were run out; 12 (2.74%) were stumped and 3 (0.68%) hit their own wicket—what a way to go! Of the 13 stumped, 5 were from Pakistan.

On 48 occasions (0.90%) the batsmen remained frustratingly unbeaten—so near and so far from the glory of a Test hundred.

Arguably the greatest hitter of all time, Gilbert Jessop hit 93 runs for England against South Africa at Lord's in 1907 in only 75 minutes. Joe Hardstaff Jr scored 94 also in 75 minutes (for England against India at Manchester in 1936). These represent perhaps the quickest nineties in Test history.

The greatest number of fours hit by a batsman making a ninety is 19 by Clive Lloyd when scoring 95 for the West Indies against England at Kingston in 1980–81. Harry Trott (Australia), Hanumant Singh (India) and Roy Dias (Sri Lanka) hit 18 fours each when registering their nineties.

In contrast, Pakistan's Taslim Arif could manage only four fours during his 90 against India at Calcutta in 1979-80 after defending for 424 minutes. The slowest ninety, however, came from India's normally attacking batsman M.L. Jaisimha who took 504 minutes to score 99 (with 12 fours against Pakistan at Kanpur in 1960–61), crawling at 11.78 runs per hour.

Australia's Sam Loxton hit most sixes, five, when scoring 93 against England at Leeds in 1948, which came in 132 minutes and off 127 balls. Another Australian, Rod Marsh, belted four sixes and nine fours in his 91 against England at Manchester in 1972. England's Keith Fletcher, known for his defensive tactics both as a batsman and a manager, surprised team-mates and spectators by hammering four sixes and 10 fours during his unbeaten 97 against India at Madras in 1972–73.

The following batsmen hit three sixes each when scoring their 90s: the West Indian opener Gordon Greenidge in his Test debut in 1974–75, Mohinder Amarnath and Krish Srikkanth of India in 1982–83 and 1988–89 respectively,

Kim Hughes made three 90s including a 99 at Perth in 1979–80. (Ken Piesse library)

Grim-faced Mickey Stewart (manager) and Mike Gatting (captain) watch England lose a Sydney Test in 1987. Gatting's 96 brought England close to a thrilling win.

India's Ravi Shastri relaxing with a young fan on the SCG. Overnight not out on 95, he compiled a historic 209 in Sydney in 1992. He remembers his 93 in the Delhi Test with mixed feelings.

Pakistani great Imran Khan in 1991–92, and Duleep Mendis of Sri Lanka in 1984.

Mendis' 94 came off only 96 balls and India's record-breaking all-rounder Kapil Dev's 98 off 98 balls in 1982–83.

The prize for scoring the most spectacular ninety should, however, go to the Kiwi knight Richard Hadlee whose 99 came off only 81 balls and in 111 minutes at Christchurch in 1983–84, and included 18 fours.

Andy Ganteaume, the diminutive deputy wicket-keeper for the West Indies, was a happy man when he scored 112 on his debut in the 1947–48 Port-of-Spain Test against England. Surprisingly, he was never picked again—a 'second wicket-keeper dropsy syndrome.' But at least he had the consolation of scoring a Test hundred, not to mention an average of 112.00—superior to Bradman's 99.94. (Whoever said 'there are liars, bloody liars and statisticians' is bang-on target in the above case.)

Vic Stollmeyer, the elder brother of Jeff (who regularly opened for the West Indies), had no such consolation. Vic was stumped for 96 runs scored in 150 minutes in his only Test appearance, against England at The Oval in 1939. Then came World War II, which started less than two weeks later, and it was bye-bye Victor and welcome back Jeff who hit four centuries in 32 Tests without the trauma of a ninety when Test cricket recommenced in 1946.

Call Vic a war casualty with a difference. Imagine being stumped for 96 in one's only Test appearance. What could be sadder?

Just ask Rick McCosker and Alan Knott. McCosker, the tall New South Wales opening batsman, was marooned on 95 in the 1975 Leeds Test against England. He was robbed of a century for a most unlikely reason. On the last morning of a well-poised Test, McCosker needed five runs for his century and Australia 225 runs for a victory with seven wickets intact. But the match was abandoned because vandals, campaigning for the release of a convicted criminal, had dug up the pitch with knives and poured oil all over it.

England's rubbery wicket-keeper, Alan Knott, was four runs short of his maiden Test hundred when rioting in Pakistan compelled the abandonment of the final Test in Karachi in March 1969. Surely, the rioters could have waited for 10 minutes!

The great Ranjitsinhji ran out of time in the last innings (v. Australia at Nottingham in 1899) with a century only seven runs away and 'tantalisingly beckoning'.

To quote Phill Cartwright from his booklet *90+: A Study of Scores of 90–99 in Test Cricket*: 'These then are men who fell in their nervous nineties, victims—they might tell you—of thoughtless partners, ruthless skippers, rain, time, vandals, rioters, flukes, "inept" umpires, amazing fielding, miraculous catches and occasionally—just occasionally—plain nerves, a bad shot or a good ball.'

He should have added: fielders with baseball arms, opposing captains with a degree in psychology and, as in the case of Vic Stollmeyer, forgetful, unappreciative selectors.

Finally, a word for the courageous umpires who have made a close decision against a home batsman in the nineties when the heart and a partisan crowd would have preferred an 'I saw nothing' attitude. The West Indies umpire who gave Test debutant Bob Christiani out lbw for 99 against England at Bridgetown in 1947–48 was wildly jeered by the home crowd.

This antagonism was nothing compared to what the Windies umpire P. Burke went through in the Kingston Test of 1953–54. Physical attacks were made on his wife and son by a section of the crowd when he upheld an lbw appeal by Brian Statham against local player John Holt when he was 94 in his first Test.

Thus a ninety can be nervous, sad, noble, negligent, inspiring, exasperating *and* violent.

6 499 Run Out and Other Cri-gedies

To some a century is only a stepping stone, a mere warm-up and scores of 190s and 290s are but missed milestones.

There are batsmen who occasionally throw away their wickets after reaching their hundred. Victor Trumper, Keith Miller, Denis Compton, David Gower, Neil Harvey, Frank Worrell, Viv Richards, Ian Botham, Mark Waugh…would say 'enough is enough' and give away their wicket to a deserving bowler once they were convinced that their stay in the middle was not vital to the team.

Then there are the run-gluttons; Bill Ponsford, Don Bradman, Wally Hammond, George Headley, Vijay Hazare, Len Hutton, Geoff Boycott, Hanif Mohammad, Sunil Gavaskar, Zaheer Abbas, Graham Gooch, David Boon, Brian Lara…who would take fresh guard at 100, then reach 200, take guard again and would kick themselves if they played a careless shot after hours in the sun. To them a century is only a stepping stone, a mere warm-up for their full-frontal attack on the bowling, and scores of 190s and 290s are missed milestones.

Martin Crowe, the graceful New Zealand batsman, was so devastated to be dismissed for 299 against Sri Lanka in the 1991 Wellington Test that he groaned: 'It's a bit like climbing Everest and pulling a hamstring in the last stride. It would have been great to get 300. I was angry about it but then I settled down.'

His marathon 299 in the second innings was far from being a selfish indulgence. Dismissed for a paltry 174 in the first knock, the Kiwis faced a deficit of 323 runs. Crowe *had* to dig himself in and bat the whole day. He did more than that. He batted for 610 minutes, faced 523 deliveries, hit 29 fours and three sixes and added 467 runs for the third wicket with Andrew Jones. It remains the highest partnership for any wicket in Test cricket, and it saved New Zealand from a humiliating defeat.

But with only three balls remaining in the Test and Crowe needing just a single for his triple ton, he was caught behind. Even the toiling Sri Lankans were disappointed.

Bradman was equally keen to get his 300 in the Adelaide Test against South Africa in 1931–32. A Test triple century had not been recorded on an Australian ground before then, and the Don badly wanted that achievement on his CV. He was on 284 when joined by last man Hugh 'Pud' Thurlow—a fast bowler from Queensland. Farming the strike, Bradman reached 298. Then a shot to the leg made them go for two but Thurlow could not make his ground and was run out. It was a double tragedy as Bradman remained 299 not out and Thurlow made a duck in what proved to be his only Test.

Bradman had scored 334 against England at Leeds only a year earlier, and chalked another triple hundred, 304, on the same ground in 1934. Still, the missed landmark at Adelaide must have rankled the great run-machine—especially later on when Australia's Bob Cowper hit 307 against England at Melbourne in 1965–66.

Mohammad Azharuddin made two 'super nineties' in Test cricket: 199 and 192. Here he is seen executing his famous backfoot drive on the MCG. (Ken Piesse library)

India's little-known Shantanu Sugwekar provided another instance of scoring a near triple ton in a first-class match. He registered an unbeaten 299 in a Ranji Trophy match for Maharashtra against Madhya Pradesh at Pune in 1989. Among the bowlers he faced were leg-spinner Narendra Hirwani (who had captured 16 for 136 in his spectacular Test debut against the Windies in Madras the previous season) and off-spinner Rajesh Chauhan who later represented India in Tests.

By coincidence, Punjab's Gurusharan Singh scored 298 not out in a Ranji Trophy quarter-final match against Bengal at Calcutta only a fortnight later. Despite Gurusharan's gallant effort, his team (551 runs) lost to Bengal (594) on first innings, a dual disappointment for the Sikh.

The following batsmen have carried their bats through a completed innings while scoring 99 or 199 in first-class cricket:

Batsman	Score/ Team Total	For	Against	Venue	Year
G. Ulyett	199*/399	Yorkshire	Derbyshire	Sheffield	1887
N. Claxton	199*/378	S. Australia	Victoria	Victoria	1905–06
A.E. Dipper	99*/185	Gloucestershire	Worcestershire	Cheltenham	1919
P.E. Whitelaw	99*/183	Auckland	M.C.C.	Auckland	1936–37
W.W. Keeton	99*/190	Nottinghamshire	Kent	Nottingham	1937
A.H. Dyson	99*/196	Glamorgan	Gloucestershire	Newport	1939
L. Hutton	99*/200	Yorkshire	Leicestershire	Sheffield	1948
G. Boycott	99*/215	England	Australia	Perth (Test match)	1979–80

* = Not out

Ulyett's and Claxton's scores were their highest in their first-class careers. 'One wonders whether they were disappointed at just missing out on their double century or were happy to have carried their bat,' commented cricket-fan Graham Clayton from New South Wales who sent me this information.

Alan Wharton, Lancashire's left-handed middle-order batsman, played one Test for England in 1949 but injury deprived him of another chance. His claim to fame was his 199 run out in six hours against Sussex at Hove in 1959, which remained his highest score.

For want of a better term, I have described scores from 190 to 199, 290 to 299, etc. as 'Super Nineties'. Such Super Nineties in Test cricket are listed in the Appendix. Once again, an Australian, Clem Hill, is the pioneer in this ultra-exclusive club, hitting 191 against South Africa in Sydney in 1910–11.

So far, 27 batsmen have recorded Super Nineties in Test history. Five have achieved it twice; they are West Indians Everton Weekes, Frank Worrell and Vivian Richards, Australia's Ian Chappell and India's Mohammad Azharuddin. Venue-wise, Lord's and The Oval have witnessed the Super Nineties most often, four times each, followed by Sydney, Adelaide and Kanpur, three times each.

Only four batsmen have reached Super-99 status; Bradman 299 not out in 396 minutes, Crowe 299 in 610 minutes, Pakistan's Mudassar Nazar 199 in 522 minutes and Azharuddin 199 in 500 minutes. It just shows how fast Bradman batted.

Surprisingly, no one has made a score in 390s in first-class cricket. However, this brings us to the Mount Everest of tall-scoring, Hanif Mohammad's 499, which remained a World Record until the West Indies' great Brian Lara amassed 501 not out in England on 6 June 1994.

After batting for 640 minutes (that is, almost 11 hours) Hanif was run out when going for his 500th run! This record-cruncher was played for Karachi against Bahawalpur in the semi-final of Qaid-I-Azam Trophy in Karachi in January 1959. The 24-year-old hit 64 fours and overtook Bradman's 29 year-old record of 452 not out (compiled in only 415 minutes, with 49 fours, for New South Wales against Queensland in Sydney in January 1930).

Bahawalpur totalled 185, Karachi replied with 7 declared for 772 (apart from Hanif, Test cricketer Wallis Mathias scored 103 and was run out too, Hanif's elder brother Wazir was stumped for 31 and younger brother Mushtaq made 21). Bahawalpur were wiped out for 108 in the second innings and lost by an innings and 479 runs.

The memory of that match must be still haunting the brave Bahawalpurians. But the mystery is: what madness struck the level-headed Hanif? Imagine, concentrating for 640 minutes and then to throw it all away when a single short of a unique quintuple century.

There are several versions of Hanif's dismissal. One states that he was 499 and was run out when going for his 500th run off the last ball of the day. Another account, as given by the well-known statistician Irving Rosenwater in Pakistan's *The Cricketer Spring Annual* (1959), states that Hanif was 498 and was run out while taking the second run off the last ball of the third day, 11 January 1959.

A third version says that Hanif, on 497, attempted a quick single off the last ball off the second-last over so that he could get the 500th run in the final over. When he was run-out, he thought he was 497, according to this account, because the scoreboard indicated that figure. Only on returning to the pavilion did he discover that he had made 499.

Which one is true?

To give details from Rosenwater's research: On 8 January, Bahawalpur were dismissed for 185 shortly after tea on the opening day. At stumps, Karachi were 59 for no loss, Hanif 25. Against a weakened Bahawalpur attack in the absence of their best bowler, Shahnawaz, Hanif added 230 to his score on the second day. To quote Rosenwater: 'the true brilliance of his batting was seen. Not for a minute did he lose concentration…while boundary upon boundary flowed from his bat.'

Such was his domination that, of the 275 runs added for the second and third wickets, Hanif scored more that 200 while his partners including Wazir Mohammad, elder brother and captain, 'watched in an almost silent admiration.'

Having reached his century in 160 minutes, he accelerated to score his next hundred in only 102 minutes. At stumps on day two he had hit 31 fours and was unbeaten on 255 with Karachi 3 for 383. His individual score was already a tournament record.

The next day was a rest day and the match was resumed on Sunday, 11 January. It was Hanif's day as he broke Bradman's world record, adding 244 to his overnight score. Pakistan's 'Little Master' raced past his triple ton before lunch, and at tea was on 435, just 17 runs short of Bradman's record. Rosenwater continues:

'This was duly passed and indeed Hanif continued his relentless way. With one ball of the day remaining for play, his total stood (almost incredibly) at 498, and the desire to reach the fabulous figure of 500 must have been irresistible. In the event he was run out trying to turn a single into a 2, and he walked off the field having made 499.'

He had been associated in three century partnerships: 172 for the second wicket with Waqar Hassan, 103 for the third wicket with brother Wazir and 259 for the fourth wicket with Wallis Mathias.

Bradman was among the first to send congratulations to Hanif. The then President of Pakistan, General Mohammed Ayub Khan, also

HANIF'S 499 RUN OUT

Karachi, Jan. 8 - 12, 1959

BAHAWALPUR

First Innings

			Second Innings	
Ijaz Hussain run out	24		c Waqar b Mahmood	32
Zulfiqar Ahmed c Aziz b Mahmood	0		c Aziz b Mahmood	8
Mohammad Iqbal b Ikram	20		c Aziz b Munaf	0
Mohammad Ramzan c Wallis b Ikram	64		lbw b Munaf	5
Ghiasuddin b Ikram	4		c Wazir b Ikram	12
Jamil Khalid run out	12		b D'Souza	4
Farrukh Salim c Aziz b Mahmood	3		b Ikram	4
Riaz Mahmood b Mahmood	4		lbw b Mushtaq	10
Asad Bhatti st Aziz b Mushtaq	21		b Ikram	4
Tanvir Hussan not out	16		c Aziz b D'Souza	7
Aziz Ahmed b Ikram	8		not out	5
Extras	9		Extras	17
	185			108

KARACHI

Hanif Mohammad run out	499
Alim-ud-din c Zulfiqar b Aziz	32
Waqar Hassan c Tanvir b Iqbal	37
Wazir Mohammad st Tanvir b Jamil	31
Wallis Mathias run out	103
Mushtaq Mohammad lbw b Aziz	21
Abdul Munaf b Iqbal	18
Abdul Aziz not out	9
Extras	22
(7 wkts dec.)	772

Ikram Elahi, Mahmood Hussain and Antao D'Souza did not bat.

Hanif MOHAMMAD

Karachi Bowling

	Overs	Mdns	Runs	Wkts	Overs	Mdns	Runs	Wkts
Mahmood	18	4	38	3	10	2	27	2
Ikram	17	3	48	4	8	2	10	3
Munaf	8	1	23	—	9	1	29	2
D'Souza	11	2	42	—	11	3	17	2
Mushtaq	4	—	19	1	3	—	8	1
Hanif	1		6	—				

Bahawalpur Bowling

	Overs	Mdns	Runs	Wkts
Zulfiqar	34	5	95	—
Ramzan	19	—	83	—
Aziz	50	4	208	2
Riaz	9	—	44	—
Ghias	37	3	139	—
Jamil	23	1	93	1
Iqbal	25	3	81	2
Tanvir	3	—	7	—

Umpires: Idris Beg and Daud Khan.

sent a message of congratulations and a cash award equivalent to £75.

Which version is correct? What really happened? To solve the mystery once and for all I wrote to the noted London-based Pakistani cricket correspondent, Qamar Ahmed, who edits *Pakistan Book of Cricket*. He talked to Hanif Mohammad on my behalf.

Hanif's own version is that he was misled by the scoreboard. According to him: The scoreboard showed 496 with only two balls left for the day. To get to his 500 before the end of the day's play, he intended to take two off each ball. He played into covers, took a single and while going for the second run was run out. It was when he was back in the pavilion that he discovered that he had made 499.

So in fact he was on 498 when the scoreboard showed 496. Had he known that he would have adopted different tactics. 'Those damn fool scorers got it wrong,' Hanif said when Brian Lara broke his record.

This, then, is version number four, but as it has come from the 'horse's mouth', it appears the most genuine. Cricketers' memory may dim after 35 summers, but you cannot forget a cri-gedy of monumental proportion like 499 run out in a hurry, can you?

The sequel to this story is even sadder. In the final of the competition played against Combined Services a few days later, the Karachi wicket-keeper Abdul Aziz played his last match.

Aziz was Hanif's batting partner and was 7 not out when the latter was run out for 499 in the semi-final. He had also taken five catches and effected a stumping in that match. But against Combined Services, Aziz was struck on the left side of the chest above the heart by a rising off-break from Dildar Ahmed and fell in a heap. He died 15 minutes later on the way to the hospital. Play was suspended for a day.

This cri-gedy was recorded in the scorebook as:

Abdul Aziz retired hurt, 0, in the first innings, and, did not bat, dead, in the second.

7 Snippets Nervosa et Statistica

Whitney's Ninety

The popular quickie Mike Whitney, with a first-class batting average of 5.61, has no pretensions to be a batsman. Yet once he defied the fury of Richard Hadlee and Danny Morrison for five overs to enable Australia to draw the Melbourne Test and regain the Trans-Tasman Trophy in 1987–88.

His highest score came in a Lancashire League match at Rishton, England in 1990. For Haslingden against Rishton in the Worsely Cup, he scored—don't faint—an unbeaten 93 with two sixes and 12 fours.

'The opposition had Peter Sleep, the Aussie Test spinner,' Whit said, reliving the once-in-a-lifetime experience. 'When I went in to bat at number 7, the score was 5 for 50. Soon it became 6 for 75 when seventeen year-old Neil Grinrod joined me. We added 111 runs which broke the all-time Haslingden record for the seventh wicket. I also took 5 wickets and we won the match—a very happy feeling, mate.'

Was he disappointed to miss his one and only century?

'Mate, I was *delighted* to go so close. I rang up everyone I knew— including "Henry" Lawson whose highest score is 80. Well, my only disappointment was that my wife Debbie, who watched all my previous and future matches in England that year, missed only *this* match.'

Killer 99

When Pakistan's Maqsood Ahmed was stumped by India's Narein Tamhane off Subash Gupte for 99 in the Lahore Test of 1954–55, a spectator is reported to have died of heart failure. Another angry spectator told Tamhane that Allah's curse would descend on him. As Tamhane made a duck in that Test, the curse was to some extent effective!

A tailend batsman, the popular Michael Whitney scored 93 not out in a Lancashire League match in 1990. 'I was delighted to go so close,' he purred. (Ken Piesse library)

Bradman Immune but not Harvey

Don Bradman played 80 innings in 52 Tests but was never dismissed in the 90s, 190s and 290s. However, a duck in his final Test innings at The Oval in 1948 brought down his Test average from 101.39 to 99.94. Also, he made 299 not out in a Test against South Africa at Adelaide in 1931–32. In 338 first-class innings, the great Don compiled 117 centuries and only seven nineties; his first ninety coming in his 86th innings.

Neil Harvey's only dismissal for a ninety came, curiously, in his 99th Test innings (96 v. Pakistan at Dacca in 1959–60). Apart from that he once scored an unbeaten 92 in the Sydney Test of 1954–55 against England.

Graceful 93

The legendary Dr W.G. Grace had a careful look at his scores and found that he had made every run from 0 to 100 except 93. He desperately wanted to fill in this gap till it became an obsession with him. In a county match for Gloucestershire in 1898, he lingered on 89 and refused to run. He waited till a half volley came along which he despatched for four and promptly declared the innings closed.

Herbert Sutcliffe made every score from 0 to 140 in first-class cricket, not leaving any ninety untouched.

'Ponny' and Greg Show

There were interesting similarities between Bill Ponsford and Greg Chappell—master batsmen both. They scored centuries in their first and last Tests (Ponsford 110 in his first Test and 266 in his last; Chappell 108 and 182). Also, neither was dismissed in his nineties in Tests but both had one score of unbeaten ninety (Ponsford 92 not out; Chappell 98 not out).

Hobbs Loved South Africa, Mailey 'Loved' Woolley

All three of Jack Hobbs' Test nineties came against South Africa in South Africa; 93 not out in Johannesburg in 1909–10, 92 also in Johannesburg in 1913–14 and 97 in Durban the same season.

Australian leg-spinner Arthur Mailey had England's fluent stroke-player Frank Woolley caught in the 1921 Lord's Test for 95 and 93. These were his finest innings, according to Woolley. Similarly, New Zealand fast-medium bowler Garry Troup had Gordon Greenidge caught in the 1979–80 Christchurch Test for 91 and 97.

Hundred on Their Brain

At times, the most ineffective bowlers have dismissed well-set batsmen whose minds are occupied wholly by the thought of an approaching 100. Sunil Gavaskar's *only* wicket in his 125 Test career was that of Zaheer Abbas for 96 in the Faisalabad Test in 1978–79. Also, Victor Trumper—a sublime batsman but an innocuous bowler—dismissed two batsmen in one innings of the Johannesburg Test of 1902–03: Louis Tancred for 97 and Charles Llewellyn for 90. Nervous nineties also enabled 'rabbit' bowlers Clyde Walcott, Conrad Hunte, Jeff Stollmeyer and Graham Gooch to claim their rare victims.

Retired with Measles on 99 Not Out

This piquant title comes from Jonathan Rice's *Curiosities of Cricket*. In a Varsity match in 1912, Gerald Crutchley retired at 99 because he had contracted measles. *The Wisden Book of Obituaries* confirms this story.

Going up to Oxford, 21-year-old Gerald Edward Victor Crutchley set up a curious record against Cambridge University on 8 July 1912, at Lord's. 'Having scored 99 not out, he was found at the end of the day to be suffering from measles and had to withdraw from the match.'

Wisden 1913 devotes two pages to this remarkable match: 'After a strenuous fight [both Oxford and Cambridge scoring 221 runs in the first innings], Cambridge won by three wickets…G.E.V. Crutchley scored 99 not out for Oxford on the first day, but at the end of the day was found to be suffering from an attack of measles. He could of course take no further part in the match…He was very unwell before the game began, but naturally had no idea what was the matter with him. It was stated that while he was scoring his 99 not out, his temperature went up two degrees…But for his illness, however, he would have reached three figures easily enough. He played in brilliant style…hitting ten 4's.'

Ten days before the Varsity match, Crutchley had scored 98 not out for Oxford against MCC at Lord's. That season, the two top batsmen for Oxford, R.O. Lagden and Crutchley, had each made 99 not out as their highest score.

For five years from 1957, Crutchley was President of Middlesex Cricket Club. As a lieutenant in the Scots Guard during World War I, he was wounded and held as a prisoner of war in Germany for four years. He died in August 1969, aged 78.

'Sunny' Side of Ninety

When I asked the great Indian batsman Sunil 'Sunny' Gavaskar whether he felt nervous when in the nineties, he replied: 'I don't know. I *never* look at the scoreboard when batting.'

All the same, he scored five nineties in 125 Tests including 96 in his final Test innings. (He also hit 34 Test centuries—a record by far.)

99 Cramped His Style

David Bridge finished his first-grade career with four centuries in the Illawarra District Competition in NSW. 'Yet, it was my 99 for Wollongong City against Balgownie on 31 January 1987 which stands out as the most memorable innings of my career.'

Captaining Wollongong City, he went in to bat at one wicket down for no score in the first over and was the ninth man out at 309 in the last over.

'Going in to the last over of the day, our number 11 bat Mick Keevers, fresh as a daisy, said the seven runs I needed for my ton to be a "picnic". I didn't agree as I felt exhausted. Off the last ball, needing three for my century, I pulled a short ball to the boundary which just stopped inside the boundary fence. On turning for the third run, I got cramps in both my legs. My efforts to run that final 22 metres were later described as hilarious. Keevers kept yelling at me to run but my legs gave out on me. I literally fell about a metre short and was run out for 99.

'Initially I felt terribly disappointed but as time has gone by, my wife (who witnessed that innings), team-mates and I look back and have a laugh. To add to my woe, I was told at the Club later on that I didn't qualify for a century-maker's jug of amber fluid.'

Sound of Snores

Sri Lankan batsman Ravi Ratnayeke waited 65 hours for his maiden Test century—but in vain. He was 93 not out at stumps on the opening day of the Kanpur Test against India in 1986–87. It rained heavily the next day and play was washed out. The following day was rest day which added to Ravi's anxiety.

After three practically sleepless nights, Ravi came out to bat. All he needed were seven measly runs. But come the third ball, no addition to his score, an appeal for lbw, the umpire's raised finger and a tragic figure returned to the pavilion—almost in a trance. Soon the dressing room was alive with the sound of snores.

Edrich's 96-Phobia

England's left-handed opening batsman John Edrich recorded a 'hat-trick' with a difference. In 77 Tests, he made three nineties: 96, 96 and 96. (He scored 12 centuries as well.)

Tale of Two Nineties

At stumps on 6 February 1974, in the Port-of-Spain Test against the West Indies, England's opening batsmen Denis Amiss and Geoff Boycott were both unbeaten in the nineties—the first such instance in Test history. Amiss progressed from 92 to 174 the next day but Boycott could add only two runs to his overnight 91.

Nervous 900s

No batsman has scored 1000 runs in a Test series. Don Bradman comes closest, with 974 runs at 139.14 against England in 1930. Wally Hammond is next with 905 runs at 113.12 for England v Australia in 1928–29.

99 in Both Innings

Amay Khurasiya of Madhya Pradesh, India, is the first—and so far the only—batsman to score 99 in both innings of a first-class match. He made 99 and 99 not out in a Ranji Trophy match for Madhya Pradesh against Viderbha at Nagpur in 1991–92. 'Madhya Pradesh *won* the match with Khurasiya just one run short of a century. I did *not* declare the innings closed,' explained skipper Sandeep Patil, a former Test cricketer.

Three Consecutive Nineties

India's A.G. Kripal Singh came close to it but Somerset's Mervyn Kitchen achieved it 16 years later. Kripal scored 98 and 97 in a Ranji Trophy semi-final match in 1954–55, followed by 75 and 91 in the final for Madras against Holkar, thus getting three nineties in four innings. Kitchen went one better, scoring a 'hat-trick' of nineties in 1971.

In between, in August 1948, Lancashire's John Ikin scored 99s in successive matches but not innings. He made 99 v. Essex at Blackpool and 9 and 99 v. the touring Australians at Old Trafford, Manchester. Ikin, who played 18 Tests for England from 1946 to 1955, was pleased with his odd sequence of 'five nines-in-a-row'.

More Nineties Oddities

In his splendid first-class career, the elegant Frank Woolley made, apart from his 145 first-class centuries, 35 nineties—probably the most by a batsman.

P.R. Johnson scored 98 not out and 96 not out for Somerset against Sussex, his partners twice failing him in his hour of need. An exasperating run of nineties was suffered by Aussie great Charles Macartney in 1913, when in successive innings for NSW he scored 125 and 94 v. South Australia, 94 and 76 not out against Victoria and 91 v. Rest—all on the Sydney Cricket Ground. In one season, 1949, the exuberant Laurie Fishlock made 95, 92, 91 and 91 for Surrey.

97 on Debut at 42

When playing for Boland against Border in South Africa in 1980–81, Jerry Kennedy scored 97 on his debut at the age of 42. He is probably the oldest debutant to be dismissed in the nineties.

99 in County Debut

Lancashire batsman J.J. Broughton had the misfortune to be out for 99 in his county debut against Essex at Leyton on 19 July 1901. Going in at the fall of the fifth wicket, Broughton helped Hallox to add 207 for the sixth wicket in only 145 minutes. Broughton was lucky, though, giving chances at 15 and 33. From 90 he raced to 98 with two fours. Then at 98 he got his third 'life'. But would he learn? He lashed out to drive Mead and was caught at point. It remained the only double-figure score of his career. In 1928, E.F. Wilson was dismissed for 99 on his debut for Surrey against Northamptonshire.

Nonagenarian Cricketers

No Test cricketer has yet reached 100 years in life. England's Francis Mackinnon (born 9 April 1848, died 27 February 1947) lived to only 406 days short of his 'century', the oldest ever Test cricketer. In his only Test at Melbourne in 1878 he scored 0 and 5 but he is more remembered for playing in the Varsity match in 1870 when Frank C. Cobden took his famous hat-trick. Set 179 runs to win, Oxford had made 7 for 175 when Cobden bowled his famous last over. He captured wickets off his second, third and fourth deliveries to snatch a sensational 2 run victory for Cambridge. The ball with which Cobden performed the hat-trick is kept in the Lord's Long Room in London. Mackinnon visited the Long Room every year to see the ball till he was 98. The inscription states: 'It is presumed that Cobden did the hat-trick with it'. India's cricket historian Dr Vasant Naik, however, informs me that he saw a ball at the Fenner's Museum in Cambridge with an inscription: 'The ball with which Cobden did the hat-trick.' Which is the genuine ball?

Among other nonagenarian cricketers who had previously played Test cricket are Wilfred Rhodes, 95; Sydney F. Barnes, 94; Reginald Allen ('Gubby' Allen's uncle), Hunter 'Stork' Hendry, E.J. 'Tiger' Smith and Ken Burn, 93; Percy Fender, 92; Henry Donnan, 91; Bill Ponsford, Frank, and son George, Hearne and Herbert Strudwick, 90.

Only nine first-class cricketers went past the age of 99: R. de Smidt (102 years, 253 days) for Western Province; E.A. English (102 years, 247 days) for Hampshire; J. Wheatley (102 years, 102 days) for Canterbury; Professor D.B. Deodhar (101 years, 222 days) for Maharashtra, India; G.R.U. Harman (101 years, 191 days) for Dublin University; G.O. Deane (100 years, 77 days) for Hampshire; R.H. Fowler (99 years, 317 days) for Cambridge University; H. Jenner-Fust (99 years, 89 days) for Gloucestershire; and C.L. Winser (99 years, 23 days) for South Australia.

Earache Before Heartache

David Frith, cricket author, historian and editor of *Wisden Cricket Monthly*, recalls being dismissed three times in his nineties. 'Once when playing at Trumper Park for Paddington, Sydney, around 1960, I got hit on the ear before reaching double figures, but the constant ringing in my ear did me some good that day! I reached 90 but am still smarting over being given out lbw for 95 when an off-spinner hit me high on the hip.'

Hughes' Exasperating Wait When 999

In the final Test against England at The Oval in August 1993, Merv Hughes (who had already taken more than 200 Test wickets) needed 20 runs to reach 1000 runs in his 51st Test. He scored 7 and 12, thus totalling 999 runs.

Then injury sidelined him for six Tests (against New Zealand and South Africa) in 1993–94. After sitting on the aggregate of 999 runs for 208 days, he at last got a single in the controversial Johannesburg Test of March 1994.

This made him the tenth cricketer after Ray Lindwall and Richie Benaud (Australia), Ian Botham (England), Garry Sobers and Malcolm

Marshall (West Indies), Richard Hadlee (New Zealand), Kapil Dev (India), and Imran Khan and Abdul Qadir (Pakistan) to achieve the rare double of 1000 runs and 200 wickets.

Hey, Hey, It's 199 on Saturday

Ken Norris, a Northern Districts Cricket Association player, scored 199 for the now defunct Rivington Club in Sydney in a second-grade match on a Saturday in 1959. 'I think this is a remarkable score for a Saturday afternoon match and we were all disappointed that he missed his 200,' recalls Keith M. Ross who represented NDCA till 1974 aged 54. Graeme White, the current secretary of NDCA, confirmed this story and added that Norris had also taken 38 wickets at 12.23 that season (1958–59)—including two hat-tricks.

No 99 in 37 Years

Dr Vasant Naik brings to our notice that no batsman ever got out for 99 in the communal cricket tournaments—Triangular, Quadrangular and Pentangular—played over 37 years in Bombay, India, from 1907 to 1944.

90 Run Out Wrecks Weekes' Century Spree

Everton Weekes, the Windies great, had an amazing sequence of five centuries in four consecutive Tests: 141 v. England at Kingston 1948–49, 128 at Delhi, 194 at Bombay and 162 and 101 at Calcutta—the last four tons were against India. Then in the next Test at Madras, he was run out for 90, to end the unique sequence. Spectators could not believe what their eyes had seen. Nor could Weekes, who thought that he was well within the crease!

Slashing Wit

Alan Davidson recalls an amusing anecdote involving Hanif Mohammad and Ken 'Slasher' Mackay. Mackay was bowling to Hanif during a 1959 tour match in Pakistan and was convinced that in one over he had Hanif plumb lbw twice and caught behind once. But the Pakistani umpire knocked back all three appeals.

At the end of the over, Mackay went to field at square leg near the umpire and said: 'I bet you were umpiring when Hanif made his 499 recently.'

Umpire: 'As a matter of fact, I was, Mr Mackay, and do you know he was run out going for his 500th run?'

Mackay: 'No, I didn't know that but I bet you were umpiring at the other end.'

Not Just up His Alley

Like New South Wales' 209 cm (6' 10") tall fast bowler Phil Alley, his father Kingsley considered himself more of a bowler, with several trophies in the cabinet for taking hat-tricks. He once took all 10 wickets in an innings. Kingsley played in grade matches for Orange District Cricket in NSW (with and against the likes of Steve Bernard and Peter Toohey). He had a few scores in the seventies and eighties but no century because 'I had a tendency to go for my shots from ball one.'

However, during his final match in Queensland, when playing in the A Grade Church Union Competition in 1975, things promised to be different. The team was terribly weakened because of Christmas holidays and he had to open the batting, 'simply because no-one else wanted to,' recalls Kingsley, who was then pastor of his church.

As his colleagues were 'conscripted for this match' and were utter novices with the bat, Kingsley had to score in twos and fours (even hitting one six) and was not confident enough to take a single until the sixth ball of each over. Thus he lost about 30 to 40 runs.

With the ninth wicket down someone signalled he was on 96. 'Here was my great chance!' Kingsley recalled. 'The medium pacer looked easy enough, so I waited for the right ball to pound back over his head to the vacant spot on the boundary. It came! Mustering my last reserves of strength after two hours at the crease, I straight drove the red sphere upwards with a sense of great impending accomplishment.'

But the bowler leaped in the air like a circus contortionist, deflected the ball up in his outstretched hand—à la John Dyson in the Sydney Test of 1982—and dived back to claim an incredible catch. Kingsley was the last man out for 96. The opportunity never came again.

'I guess I'll have to leave it to my youngest son, Phil, to achieve what I could not,' he added philosophically.

Conflict of Interest

For Brett Day, it was a day to remember and regret. When batting for Seaview High School against Adelaide High in a Year 10 match in March 1993, Brett cruised along merrily, belting 18 fours and two sixes.

'Then I heard I was on 97 and went all tense. I had never made 50 before, let alone a ton. I nicked two singles to put me on 99. I reminded my father, who was the coach/umpire, of his promise to buy me a new bat if I made 100.'

'Adelaide High put on a new bowler and my father umpired at the bowler's end. First ball of the over I tried to flick off my pads to fine leg, but I missed it and the fielders appealed casually. I didn't even take any notice but my dad gave me out lbw. My team mates thought it was hilarious, but it took me about three weeks to see the funny side of it.'

Brett had thus missed out on both a century and a new bat—in one ball.

Deano's Double Whammy

Dean Jones, arguably the best limited-overs batsman from Australia, twice narrowly missed centuries in Benson & Hedges World Series Cup matches. He scored 99 not out (in 77 balls, with three sixes) against Sri Lanka at Adelaide on 28 January 1985. Nine years later, in the first match of his comeback, he hit 98 against South Africa at Brisbane on 9 January 1994. In all he has made six nineties in limited over internationals, a record he shares with New Zealand's Martin Crowe.

Horror Run Outs in Auckland

Australian spinner Kerry O'Keeffe had his moment as a batsman in a match against Auckland in Auckland in February 1974. On 99, he looked forward to his first ever ton when number 11 bat Ashley Mallett was run out. O'Keeffe never got so close to a century again, he remembers with regret. Oddly, the Australians totalled 399 in that innings. 'I was 81 not out with a day to go,' O'Keeffe recalled. 'Ian Chappell could have declared but he batted on to give me a chance to get my maiden hundred. I went from 81 to 99 easily, then pushed the ball wide at cover to Mark Burgess. He picked up the ball brilliantly and to my horror and acute disappointment, ran out Ashley.'

Another bowler, the New Zealand quickie Gary Bartlett was on his way to his maiden first-class hundred (for Central District v. Auckland in 1959–60). As he ran for his 100th run, the last man in, Ian Colquhoun, suddenly pulled up with a leg injury and was run out. Bartlett was left stranded on 99 not out which remained his highest first-class score.

Dean Jones in a pensive mood. He hit six nineties in limited-over internationals (LOI), a record he shares with Martin Crowe. Jones is one of three batsmen to make an unbeaten 99 in LOIs. (Ken Piesse library)

Gotcha! Merv Hughes, the mean quickie, can handle a bat too. He is among ten cricketers to achieve the 1000 runs, 200 wickets Test double. He had a seven month wait going from 999 runs to 1000. (Ken Piesse library)

Gavin's Agony

Apart from Kerry O'Keeffe, Gavin Robertson—the lanky ever-smiling NSW and Australian off-spinner—is the only Australian to score a 99 without recording a first-class century although it may be added that Robertson's career is far from over. His agonising moment came in March 1991 when he represented Tasmania against NSW at Hobart in the Sheffield Shield.

'In reply to NSW's 502, Tasmania were 8 for 532 at stumps on the third day,' remembers Gavin. 'I was unbeaten on 88 when the final day began. It was my last match for Tasmania and I was flying back to Sydney with the NSW boys so I wanted to do something special. I had already put on 156 runs for the seventh wicket with Rod Tucker [who made 165] in little over three hours. Then with Stuart Oliver I ran eight quick singles to reach 96 when Stuart got out. Tim Bower at number 11 was shaky and was lucky to be given not out when clearly out. Good omen for me, I thought.

'When on 97, came "Cracker" [Wayne Holdsworth] with the new ball. The first ball was real quick, it touched my pad and raced for 4. I pretended it was off my bat to get my hundred but the umpire correctly signalled it as a leg-bye. The next ball was short and sharp, I connected and ran two to go to 99. I blocked the next one but the fourth one bowled me.

'I heard the stumps rattle and was devastated. Bowled for 99 by my friend "Cracker", with whom I had sharpened my cricketing skill at the Bill Madden Coaching nets in Sydney.'

Run, Brother; Don't Run

Bernard Ryan's luck ran out three times in 1936 at crucial times. When representing Parramatta's first-grade cricket club, he had the misfortune of getting run out twice, when 97 and 98.

Then came the ultimate tear-jerker, the nadir of his cricket career. He was on 99 when his brother Frank, with a view to give him strike, ran him out. To be run out for 97, 98 and 99 in one season made Bernard react violently.

First, he knocked the stumps over with his bat, then flung the bat to the ground, peeled off his gloves, removed his cap, threw all these on the ground and stalked off the field in a huff, remembers his guilt-ridden brother Frank almost 60 years later:

'No one said a word. One of our team members came out, collected the mess and returned to the pavilion as the umpire turned a blind eye.'

Nine Nineties for the Mohammads

The four Mohammad brothers recorded seven nineties (apart from 29 centuries) in Test cricket: Wazir 97 not out, Hanif 96 and 93, Mushtaq 99, Sadiq 91, 98 not out and 97. Hanif's son, Shoaib, scored 94 and 95 in Tests—making it a cool nine nineties in the family. At times it seems that Test nineties run in families. Dave Nourse and son Dudley made two nineties each for South Africa; Walter Hadlee one and son Richard two for New Zealand; Vijay Manjrekar two and son Sanjay one for India; and Vinoo Mankad and son Ashok one each for India.

Fictional Nineties

Barbara Feldon, the heroine of the television series *Get Smart*, has no name except Ninety-Nine. The bumbling Maxwell Smart (played by Don Adams) also calls his fellow-spy—and later his wife—nothing but Ninety-Nine.

Then there was the Australian TV sex-soapie *No. 96* in the 1970s, which changed our viewing habits. Naughty ninety-six was how the reviewers described it.

In literature, humorist P.G. Wodehouse (who lived to be 93) created Mike Jackson based on one of the famous Foster brothers of Worcestershire. Wodehouse's story of Jackson bowled for 98 when a rich patron, Mr Bickersdyke, walked behind the bowler's arm brought forth many sighs and guffaws in his novel *Psmith in the City*, which was published in 1910.

Holmes and Away

L.H. Coulson of Hull, England, was a little boy when he saw the famous English cricketer Percy Holmes score 199 for Yorkshire against Somerset in July 1923. 'I can still remember the look on his face when he returned to the pavilion,' recalled Mr Coulson, 71 years later.

'When Holmes became a cricket coach at Scarborough College in Yorkshire, I asked my son (who was a student there) to ask Percy if he remembered the incident. He replied that he had never forgotten it.' That was in 1953, 30 years after his 199.

New Year Blues

Peter Terrey of Castle Cove, NSW, played up to second-grade cricket with the Northern District Cricket Club for 12 years in the 1960s and

1970s. His personal sob-story took place in a fourth grade match against Manly on New Year's Day, 1969.

In reply to Manly's 188, Terrey and partner took the score to 174 when he was run out from the bowler's end for 99. Later, Terrey discovered to his chagrin that the scorers had taken a single off his score to balance the bowler's analysis when he was in his eighties. 'I have always believed that the batsman's score would more likely be correct and it remains a mystery to me why I did not protest,' Terrey opined.

After his departure his team, chasing 189 for a win, collapsed from 1 for 174 to 7 for 187 and the match ended in a nail-biting draw.

'Certainly I would have preferred to reach three figures,' Terry says, but there is no doubting I have recalled that innings of 99 many more times than the two centuries I did score in my modest career.'

Lucky Loxton

Two unrelated Loxtons scored centuries on their first-class debut; Sam a double hundred for Victoria and John a round 100 for Queensland against Western Australia at Perth in 1966–67. Actually, when John F.C. Loxton was dismissed, he thought he had scored 99 as shown on the scoreboard. His depression was lifted when the scorers later realised that a run had been wrongly credited to his partner which gave him a century on debut.

To Hundred and Back

Max Benjamin, a grade cricketer from Petersham Club in Sydney, had a contrasting experience. He played in the final of the first-grade competition against St George on the Sydney Cricket Ground in 1961, which was televised on the ABC.

Benjamin was 97 when he hit a ball to deep mid-wicket. It was signalled a four which took him to 101 and this figure was registered on the scoreboard. However, after a conference it was established that the ball was stopped inside the boundary and his score was reduced by two. In the same over, he was caught by St George's Vic Michael for 99.

McNeilly Ruins Reed's Ton Party on SCG

First-class cricket umpire Graham Reed once hit a century for Sydney University in first-grade competition and 20 centuries in the City and Suburban competition for I. Zingari and other clubs.

But rather than these hundreds, he recalls a 99 he scored some 25 summers ago.

Captaining the Combined City & Suburban XI against the New South Wales Cricket Association XI (made up of Sydney's first-grade and Sheffield Shield players) on the Sydney Cricket Ground in March 1969, Reed won the toss and opened the batting. When on 98, Billy Watson, the former NSW and Australian Test cricketer, walked past him and whispered: 'Reedie, next over I'll bowl you a slow half-volley outside the off stump and you do the rest.'

Next over, Dick French, who later became a Test umpire, nudged a single. 'And there I was facing Billy Watson,' Reed recalled. 'True to his word, he bowled me a slow half-volley and I cracked a perfect cover-drive—even if I say so myself—to deep cover point towards the old Brewongle Stand. Dick and I went through the first run quickly. There seemed two in it but I did not bargain on the fact that I had hit the ball to Ian McNeilly—a NSW representative baseballer. Oh boy, what an arm! The ball zoomed back—fast and low—as if shot from a gun—and I was on my way back to the famous Members' Stand, 99 run out.

'From that day, 18 March 1969, till now in mid-1994, my feelings are not of disappointment. Rather, that 99 run out on the SCG was a more memorable score anyway. Friends, cricketers, officials still talk to me about it and I can remember it as if it were yesterday.'

Sydney's *Sunday Telegraph* summed it all up without emotion: 'Graham Reed scored a splendid 99 in 137 minutes. He hit a six and 12 fours and was unlucky to be run out.' The match ended in a draw, the strong opponents struggling to 7 for 85, still 14 short of Graham's individual knock.

Negligent Ninety

Warwick Franks, teacher and cricket historian from Bathurst, NSW, had twice made the finals of *Mastermind* on ABC TV in the early 1980s—his topic: Anglo-Aussie Test cricket. He remembers his 97 with joy and regret.

'I was playing for Rovers against Valley at Meadowbank in Sydney for a Northern Districts Cricket Association Competition in January, 1965. I hit four fours off Bill Coy to reach 97 but was caught the next ball.

'Truthfully, I did not even know I was so close to my first century, so you can't call it a nervous ninety, can you? Call it a negligent ninety,' he said with a painful smile.

Saturday Torture

To score a ninety when all around you are falling like nine-pins is heroic. But to make 94 when everyone else—including sundries—hit hundreds is morale-shattering. Ask T. Flynn whose Ulster Club amassed 4 for 1238 (give or take a few) against Macquarie Club in the 1870s. The score card (which does not add up) reads:

Ulster Club

J. Flynn 249
G. Mullens 247
M. Bereton 186
J. White 178
H. Brown 147
T. Flynn 94
Sundries 100

Macquarie Club
Did not bat. Conceded the game.

And who would blame them? For the non-believers, the score card is located at the NSW Cricket Association Library in Sydney. The above two Sydney Clubs played over four consecutive Saturdays some 120 years ago.

'We will never know how the Macquarie captain persuaded his side to turn out a third and fourth Saturday for yet another thrashing,' wondered historian Richard Cashman in *Cricketer* (Australia).

Wallsend's Masochistic Madness

Former New South Wales batsman Greg Geise made six nineties (including two unbeaten ones) in first-grade cricket for Wallsend District, NSW, according to keen-as-mustard club scorer Jack Brown. Greg is one of the four Wallsend batsmen to be dismissed for 99. In an Under-21 match on Wallsend Oval in 1976–77, Greg went from 91 to 99 with two fours but was caught the next ball.

Beaming with confidence after scoring 130 runs in the first innings of a second-grade match, David Hoddle was caught for 99 in the second innings. Later in his career, he made four more nineties— three of them in first grade.

Masochistic madness struck John Whitmore in 1987–88 and Kelly King in 1991–92; both were run out for 99. Kelly was in superb touch, hitting eight fours and five sixes.

Highest First-Class Score of 99

At least 37 batsmen have recorded 99 as their highest score in first-class cricket (apart from those 13 whose highest first-class score was 99 not out—see the list in the appendix). A. Appleby remains the pioneer of this 'club', scoring 99 for Lancashire v. Yorkshire at Sheffield as far back as 1871. For Oxford University against Warwickshire at Oxford in 1967, A.R. Garofall and John Jameson hit 99 runs each. It remained Garofall's highest score. J.J. Broughton of Lancashire in 1901 and P.G. Crowther for Glamorgan in 1977, made their only score of 99 in their county/first-class debut.

Hutton's Unknown Record

Cricket-lovers know that Len Hutton made 129 centuries in first-class cricket. But few know that he is probably the only batsman to score two unbeaten 99s at that level—once carrying his bat (for Yorkshire v. Leicestershire at Sheffield in 1948). He was also dismissed twice for 99.

Humpage's Missed Landmarks

It is frustrating enough to score 99 not out; more painful if you are 99, seeing the ball really well, and it rains heavily to rob you of a certain century. Geoff Humpage of Warwickshire was marooned on 99 against Leicestershire at Hinkley when rain at the tea interval forced the match to be abandoned. Had he got that elusive single, he would have had the distinction of scoring Warwickshire's 1000th first-class century, reveals David Baggett in *The Cricket Statistician* (England).

Unbeaten 99ers

There have been at least 46 centurions who have also scored 99 not out in first-class cricket. The first to do so was Surrey's Tom Hayward (v. Essex at Leyton in 1900). The great Len Hutton was the only one to do it twice—in 1946 and 1948—carrying his bat in 1948. The others to carry the bat when scoring 99 were A.E. Dipper (Gloucestershire, 1919), P.E. Whitelaw (Auckland, 1936–37), W.W. Keeton (Nottinghamshire, 1937), A.H. Dyson (Glamorgan, 1939) and Geoff Boycott for England v. Australia in the Perth Test of 1979–80. Boycott, incidentally, is the only one to notch an unbeaten 99 in Test history.

Among other well-known centurions who have made 99 not out are: C.B. Fry, Iftikhar Pataudi, Sr, Patsy Hendren, Jack Crapp, Gilbert

Parkhouse, Colin Cowdrey, Surinder Amanarth and Zaheer Abbas. Of these, Hendren, Cowdrey and Abbas hit a century of first-class centuries—as also did Hutton and Boycott.

Interesting Highlights of Unbeaten 99ers in First-class (FC) Cricket

⟨ A.H. Dyson who carried his bat (Glamorgan v. Gloucestershire, Newport, 1939) for 99, scored 120 in the second innings.

⟨ C.B. Fry's 99 in the Sussex v. Worcestershire match at Brighton in 1907 came in the second innings, following his 125 in the first. On two other occasions, he made 99 and a century in a match. Apart from these hiccups, he registered a century in both innings of a first-class match five times.

⟨ Nottingham needed 144 runs to beat Surrey at The Oval in 1901. They reached it without loss, their opening bat A.O. James left high and dry on 99.

⟨ Yorkshire's B. Leadbeater had played as a batsman since 1966 without getting near a century. Then came his chance against Kent at Scarborough in 1974 but he missed it by a cat's whisker. He was on 99 when the mandatory 100 overs ended and the innings was closed. A few years later, he did notch a hundred in a career of 241 innings and 'got the monkey off my back.'

⟨ When Parvez Mir of Pakistan Universities scored 99 not out against Punjab B at Lahore in 1974–75, A.H. Lakhani also made 99 in the same innings.

⟨ Roger Woolley's disappointment at missing out on his century by one run was neutralised by Tasmania's first ever Sheffield Shield victory (v. Western Australia at Devonport in 1978–79). Needing 357 to win, Tasmania were 6 for 187. Then keeper Woolley (99 not out) and skipper Jack Simmons (78 not out) added 172 runs for the unbroken seventh wicket to win by 4 wickets.

⟨ Kent's S.G. Hinks was going well at 99 against Sussex at Eastbourne in 1985 when rain caused the match to be abandoned and ruined Hinks' intended century celebrations.

⟨   Nawab of Pataudi, Sr, (real name Iftikhar Ali Khan) was
    unbeaten on 94 when MCC beat Cambridge University at
    Lord's in 1933. However, due to a misunderstanding between
    the scorers and the umpires, he was allowed to add five runs
    before the match was officially declared closed. One wonders
    whether the Nawab considered himself lucky or unlucky.

90-Plus Centuries in First-Class Cricket
So far, 23 batsmen have scored a century of centuries, Jack Hobbs
leading with 197 tons. Three batsmen narrowly missed out: J.W.
Hearne, 96 centuries; C.B. Fry, 94; and Gordon Greenidge, 92.

The Ultimate Sacrifice
M. Howell, the captain of Free Foresters, declared the innings closed
against Oxford University at Oxford in 1934, when he was 99 not
out. A martyr or a masochist?

Farrell Domination
Tasmania's Michael Farrell scored 96 out of a team total of 157 in his
first-class debut against New South Wales in Sydney on 11 March
1990, during a Sheffield Shield match. His score represents 61.15 per
cent of his team's total which could be a record in domination for a
batsman making ninety in his first-class debut.

Mackay Magic
Queenslander Ken Mackay, known for his painfully slow batting,
stunned all present by aggressive stroke-play when the Australians
played Middlesex at Lord's in July 1961. Promoted to open the innings,
he displayed a full range of dazzling shots on the opening day. It
looked certain that he would reach his century before lunch but he
inexplicably slowed down and was 92 at lunch. After the break, he
attacked with renewed gusto to hammer 168 with a six and 27 fours.
    When asked as to why he slowed down before lunch, he replied:
'Had I got my century before lunch, *no one* would have believed it!'

When Dougie Wanted to Chase a Dog
Cool man Doug Walters was probably the least nervous of all
cricketers—whether he was on nought or ninety. On 14 December
1974, he scored a spectacular century off the last ball of the day in the

Perth Test against England. Amid great excitement he went from 97 to 103 with a six off Bob Willis—completing 100 runs between tea and stumps in the Perth Test.

He had started his Test career with a stroke-filled 155 at Brisbane in December 1965—a week before his 20th birthday. He strode from 50 to 90 with flourish but when 94, the play was held up by a dog chased around the field by boys. Unruffled, the flamboyant teenager reached his century.

Later, when the famous Australian cricket writer Ray Robinson asked him how he felt during the dog 'invasion' when he was in his nineties, he replied: 'I'd have liked to join in the fun—with the bat!'

Come on SCG, C'mon, C'mon!

What has Melbourne got that Sydney lacks? The MCG has 'hosted' the most number of Test 99s—seven, including the first ever at the turn of the century. And Sydneysiders, despite their harbour, Opera House and the 2000 Olympics, have yet to witness a Test 99!

Appendix

NINETIES IN TEST CRICKET
(Figures accurate to 1 June 1994)

TEAM RECORDS

Country	Tests	Total nineties	Unbeaten nineties	No. of batsmen scoring nineties
Australia	539	104	10	60[a]
England	702	122	11	70
South Africa	186	38	3	26[a]
West Indies	306	82	10	36
New Zealand	226	30	2	21
India	289	50	3	27
Pakistan	212	45	7	28
Sri Lanka	53	13	2	8
Zimbabwe	7	1	0	1
Total	1260	485	48	277[a]

[a] Actually 276 batsmen have recorded 485 nineties, as Kepler Wessels scored nineties for both Australia and South Africa.

COUNTRY-WISE BREAK-UP

For	Against									
	Aus	Eng	SAf	WI	NZ	Ind	Pak	SL	Zim	Total
Aus	–	49	14	20	7	9	3	2	0	104
Eng	50	–	24	18	8	13	8	1	0	122
SAf	13	18	–	0	2	3	0	2	0	38
WI	14	32	0	–	7	23	6	0	0	82
NZ	4	12	2	1	–	4	6	1	0	30

Against

For	Aus	Eng	SAf	WI	NZ	Ind	Pak	SL	Zim	Total
Ind	10	8	0	12	7	–	8	5	0	50
Pak	8	10	0	6	5	13	–	3	0	45
SL	2	2	1	0	2	4	2	–	0	13
Zim	0	0	0	0	0	1	0	0	–	1
Total	101	131	41	57	38	70	33	14	0	485

MODES OF DISMISSAL OF TEST NINETIES

Mode of dism.	Aus	Eng	SAf	WI	NZ	Ind	Pak	SL	Zim	Total No.	% of dism.
Caught	49	54	22	41	16	33	19	8	0	242	55.38
Caught & bowled	6	5	2	2	1	2	2	0	0	20	4.58
Bowled	21	28	7	17	4	3	5	1	0	86	19.68
LBW	15	13	3	7	3	4	4	2	1	52	11.90
Stumped	0	4	0	1	1	1	5	0	0	12	2.74
Hit wicket	1	0	0	0	1	1	0	0	0	3	0.68
Run out	2	7	1	4	2	3	3	0	0	22	5.03
Total out	94	111	35	72	28	47	38	11	1	437	
Not out	10	11	3	10	2	3	7	2	0	48	(9.9)

NINETIES IN TEST CRICKET

Distribution by country

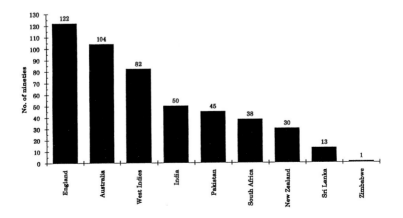

Test venues (minimum 16)

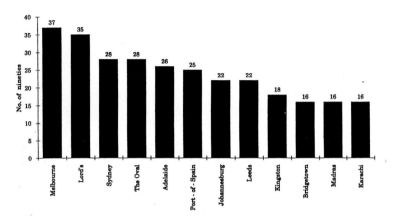

Modes of dismissal
(48 remained not out)

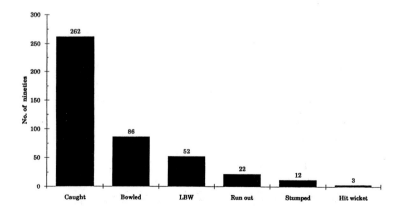

Individual nineties (minimum 5)

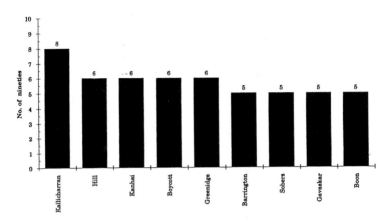

MOST INDIVIDUAL NINETIES IN TESTS

8	A.I. Kallicharran	91, 93, 98, 92*, 93, 97, 92, 98 for WI
6	C. Hill	96, 99, 98, 97, 91*, 98 for Aus
	R.B. Kanhai	96, 99, 90, 92, 90, 94 for WI
	G. Boycott	90, 92, 97, 93, 99, 99* for Eng
	C.G. Greenidge	93, 91, 96, 91, 97, 95 for WI
5	G.S. Sobers	92, 94, 95, 95*, 93 for WI
	K.F. Barrington	94, 93, 91, 93, 97 for Eng
	S.M. Gavaskar	97, 90, 90, 91, 96 for Ind
	D.C. Boon	94, 94*, 97, 93, 96 for Aus
4	E.D. Weekes	90, 90*, 94, 90 for WI
	T.W. Graveny	92, 97, 96, 96 for Eng
	P.B.H. May	91, 97, 92, 95 for Eng
	M.J.K. Smith	98, 96, 99, 99 for Eng
	M.C. Cowdrey	97, 93, 93*, 96 for Eng
	R.B. Simpson	92, 92, 91, 94 for Aus
	A.L. Wadekar	91, 99, 91*, 90 for Ind
	I.M. Chappell	96, 99, 97, 90 for Aus
	A.P.E. Knott	96*, 96, 90, 92 for Eng

R.W. Marsh   92*, 91, 97, 91 for Aus
Majid Khan   99, 98, 98, 92 for Pak
Zaheer Abbas   90, 96, 90, 91 for Pak
Javed Miandad   92, 99, 94, 92 for Pak
D.B. Vengsarkar   90, 94, 98*, 96 for Ind
J.G. Wright   93, 99, 98, 99 for NZ
A.L. Logie   97, 95*, 93, 98 for WI
K.C. Wessels   98, 90 for Aus; 95*, 92 for SAf

3   J.B. Hobbs   93*, 92, 97 for Eng
         H.W. Taylor   93, 93, 91 for SAf
         F.W. Woolley   95, 93, 95* for Eng
         E.H. Hendren   92, 95, 93 for Eng
         J. Hardstaff jr   94, 94, 98 for Eng
         L. Hutton   92, 94, 98* for Eng
         J.R. Reid   93, 92, 97 for NZ
         T. L. Goddard   90, 99, 93 for SAf
         D.C.S. Compton   93, 93, 94 for Eng
         W.M. Lawry   98, 94, 98 for Aus
         I.R. Redpath   97, 92, 93 for Aus
         K.D. Walters   93, 94*, 94 for Aus
         J.H. Edrich   96, 96, 96 for Eng
         Sadiq Mohammad   91, 98*, 97 for Pak
         R.C. Fredericks   98, 94, 98 for WI
         C.H. Lloyd   94, 91*, 95 for WI
         G.R. Viswanath   97*, 95, 96 for Ind
         M. Amarnath   90, 91, 95 for Ind
         I.V.A. Richards   98, 92, 96 for WI
         H.A. Gomes   91, 90*, 92* for WI
         G.A. Gooch   91*, 99, 93 for Eng
         K.J. Hughes   92, 99, 94 for Aus
         D.L. Haynes   96, 92, 90 for WI
         R.L. Dias   98, 97, 95 for SL
         A.R. Border   98*, 98, 91* for Aus
         J.V. Coney   92, 98, 93 for NZ
         R.B. Richardson   93, 99, 99 for WI
         S.R. Waugh   90, 91, 92 for Aus
         N.S. Sidhu   97, 99, 98 for Ind
         H.P. Tillekaratne   93, 93*, 92 for SL
         M.J. Slater   99, 92, 95 for Aus

2   53 batsmen have made two Test nineties, five of these—Geoff
         Miller (England), Derek Sealy and Deryck Murray (West Indies), and
         Chetan Chauhan and Manoj Prabhakar (India)—did not go on to
         make a Test century.

1   166 have scored one Test ninety, 57 of whom never hit a Test ton.

* = Not out

A SCORE OF 99 IN TEST CRICKET

1st inns	2nd inns	Batsman	Match	Venue	Season
15	99	C. Hill	Aus v. Eng	Melbourne	1901–02
10	99	G.A. Faulkner	SAf v. Eng	Cape Town	1909–10
99	–	C.G. Macartney	Aus v. Eng	Lord's	1912
29	99	H. Sutcliffe	Eng v. SAf	Cape Town	1927–28
99	4	A.G. Chipperfield (on Test debut)	Aus v. Eng	Nottingham	1934
99	43	E. Paynter	Eng v. Aus	Lord's	1938
22	99	N.W.D. Yardley	Eng v. SAf	Nottingham	1947
99	–	W.A. Brown	Aus v. Ind	Melbourne	1947–48
1	99	R.J. Christiani (on Test debut)	WI v. Eng	Bridgetown	1947–48
99	56	B. Mitchell	SAf v. Eng	Port Elizabeth	1948–49
44	99	K.R. Miller	Aus v. Eng	Adelaide	1950–51
99	–	A.F. Rae	WI v. NZ	Auckland	1951–52
99	44	A.R. Morris	Aus v. SAf	Melbourne	1952–53
99	–	J.E.F. Beck	NZ v. SAf	Cape Town	1953–54
99	15	Maqsood Ahmed	Pak v. Ind	Lahore	1954–55
99	–	C.C. McDonald	Aus v. SAf	Cape Town	1957–58
99	14	R.B. Kanhai	WI v. Ind	Madras	1958–59
0	99	Pankaj Roy	Ind v. Aus	Delhi	1959–60
99	–	M.J.K. Smith	Eng v. SAf	Lord's	1960
99	28	T.L. Goddard	SAf v. Eng	The Oval	1960
99	–	M.L. Jaisimha	Ind v. Pak	Kanpur	1960–61
99	34	M.J.K. Smith	Eng v. Pak	Lahore	1961–62
70	99	E.R. Dexter	Eng v. Aus	Brisbane	1962–63
99	5	R.M. Cowper	Aus v. Eng	Melbourne	1965–66
6	99	A.L. Wadekar	Ind v. Aus	Melbourne	1967–68
28	99	R.F. Surti	Ind v. NZ	Auckland	1967–68
99	–	I.M. Chappell	Aus v. Ind	Calcutta	1969–70
99	18	M.L.C. Foster	WI v. Ind	Port-of-Spain	1970–71
99	23	Majid Khan	Pak v. Eng	Karachi	1972–73
99	0	Mushtaq Mohd	Pak v. Eng	Karachi	1972–73
99	21*	D.L. Amiss	Eng v. Pak	Karachi	1972–73
99	112	G. Boycott	Eng v. WI	Port-of-Spain	1973–74
99	52*	R. Edwards	Aus v. Eng	Lord's	1975
99	4	K.J. Hughes	Aus v. Eng	Perth	1979–80
0	99*	G. Boycott	Eng v. Aus	Perth	1979–80
99	51	G.A. Gooch	Eng v. Aus	Melbourne	1979–80
99	–	Javed Miandad	Pak v. Ind	Bangalore	1983–84
99	–	R.J. Hadlee	NZ v. Eng	Christchurch	1983–84
99	–	Salim Malik	Pak v. Eng	Leeds	1987
99	43	J.G. Wright	NZ v. Aus	Melbourne	1987–88
99	–	M.D. Moxon	Eng v. NZ	Auckland	1987–88

1st inns	2nd inns	Batsman	Match	Venue	Season
15	99	R.B. Richardson	WI v. Ind	Port–of–Spain	1988–89
99	–	D.M. Jones	Aus v. NZ	Perth	1989–90
1	99	R.B. Richardson	WI v. Aus	Bridgetown	1990–91
99	6	D.N. Patel	NZ v. Eng	Christchurch	1991–92
28	99	J.G. Wright	NZ v. Eng	Christchurch	1991–92
99	–	M.E. Waugh	Aus v. Eng	Lord's	1993
80	99	M.A. Atherton	Eng v. Aus	Lord's	1993
10	99	M.J. Slater	Aus v. NZ	Perth	1993–94
99	–	N.S. Sidhu	Ind v. SL	Bangalore	1993–94

A NINETY ON TEST DEBUT

1st inns	2nd inns	Batsman	Match	Venue	Season
91	5	F.S. Jackson	Eng v. Aus	Lord's	1893
97	24	L.J. Tancred	SAf v. Aus	Johannesburg	1902–03
90	17	R.B. Minnett	Aus v. Eng	Sydney	1911–12
22	98	A.J. Richardson	Aus v. Eng	Sydney	1924–25
99	4	A.G. Chipperfield	Aus v. Eng	Nottingham	1934
93	106	P.A. Gibb	Eng v. SAf	Johannesburg	1938–39
96	–	V.H. Stollmeyer	WI v. Eng	The Oval	1939
1	99	R.J. Christiani	WI v. Eng	Bridgetown	1947–48
97	28*	F.M.M. Worrell	WI v. Eng	Port–of–Spain	1947–48
90	–	P.N.F. Mansell	SAf v. Eng	Leeds	1951
94	1	J.K. Holt	WI v. Eng	Kingston	1953–54
93	64	N.S. Harford	NZ v. Pak	Lahore	1955–56
97	25	I.R. Redpath	Aus v. SAf	Melbourne	1963–64
95	26	Abdul Kadir	Pak v. Aus	Karachi	1964–65
0	94	C. Milburn	Eng v. WI	Manchester	1966
26	90	B. Wood	Eng v. Aus	The Oval	1972
93	107	C.G. Greenidge	WI v. Ind	Bangalore	1974–75
14	92	R.W. Anderson	NZ v. Pak	Lahore	1976–77
90	46	Taslim Arif	Pak v. Ind	Calcutta	1979–80
92	75	B.M. Laird	Aus v. WI	Brisbane	1979–80
94	–	R.C. Russell	Eng v. SL	Lord's	1988
16	92	S.P. Fleming	NZ v. Ind	Hamilton	1993–94

Note: When Jack Holt was given out lbw for 94 on his home ground, his angry supporters made physical attacks on the wife and son of the 'offending' umpire. Holt made a century in the following Test. Abdul Kadir was run out in the first innings and hit his wicket in the second; Taslim Arif opened the innings, batted for 424 minutes and hit only 4 fours. It was V.H. Stollmeyer's only innings of his one-Test career.

A NINETY IN FINAL TEST

1st inns	2nd inns	Batsman	Match	Venue	Season
32	93	A. Ward	Eng v. Aus	Melbourne	1894–95
125	97	P.G.V. van der Bijl	SAf v. Eng	Durban	1938–39
96	–	V.H. Stollmeyer	WI v. Eng	The Oval	1939
99	56	B. Mitchell	SAf v. Eng	Port Elizabeth	1948–49
49	98	Imtiaz Ahmed	Pak v. Eng	The Oval	1962
35	91	B.F. Butcher	WI v. Eng	Leeds	1969
21	96	S.M. Gavaskar	Ind v. Pak	Bangalore	1986–87

Note: Five of seven scored a ninety in their final Test innings. All of these players had scored centuries before, although van der Bijl did so just in the first innings. It was Stollmeyer's only Test. Stollmeyer's and van der Bijl's Test careers were terminated by World War II.

A NINETY AND A CENTURY IN SAME TEST
(by country)

Australia: R.M. Cowper, P.M. Toohey, A.R. Border
England: P.A. Gibb (on debut), M.C. Cowdrey, K.F. Barrington, A.P.E. Knott, G. Boycott
South Africa: P.G.V. van der Bijl
West Indies: G.S. Sobers, S.M. Nurse, C.G. Greenidge (on debut)
New Zealand: —
India: C.G. Borde, M. Amarnath
Pakistan: Hanif Mohammad, Zaheer Abbas, Mohsin Khan
Sri Lanka: L.R.D. Mendis, P.A. de Silva
Zimbabwe: —

A NINETY AND A CENTURY IN THE SAME TEST
(individual scores)

1st inns	2nd inns	Batsman	Match	Venue	Season
93	106	P.A. Gibb (on debut)	Eng v. SAf	Johannesburg	1938–39
125	97	P.G.V. van der Bijl	SAf v. Eng	Durban	1938–39
109	96	C.G. Borde	Ind v. WI	Delhi	1958–59
114	97	M.C. Cowdrey	Eng v. WI	Kingston	1959–60
101	94	K.F. Barrington	Eng v. Aus	Sydney	1962–63
104	93	Hanif Mohammad	Pak v. Aus	Melbourne	1964–65
92	108	R.M. Cowper	Aus v. Ind	Adelaide	1967–68
152	95*	G.S. Sobers	WI v. Eng	Georgetown	1967–68
95	168	S.M. Nurse	WI v. NZ	Auckland	1968–69

1st inns	2nd inns	Batsman	Match	Venue	Season
101	96	A.P.E. Knott	Eng v. NZ	Auckland	1970–71
99	112	G. Boycott	Eng v. WI	Port-of-Spain	1973–74
93	107	C.G. Greenidge (on debut)	WI v. Ind	Bangalore	1974–75
90	100	M. Amarnath	Ind v. Aus	Perth	1977–78
122	97	P.M. Toohey	Aus v. WI	Kingston	1977–78
176	96	Zaheer Abbas	Pak v. Ind	Faisalabad	1978–79
94	101*	Mohsin Khan	Pak v. Ind	Lahore	1982–83
98*	100*	A.R. Border	Aus v. WI	Port-of-Spain	1983–84
111	94	L.R.D. Mendis	SL v. Eng	Lord's	1984
96	123	P.A. de Silva	SL v. NZ	Auckland	1990–91

NINETIES IN BOTH INNINGS OF A TEST

1st inns	2nd inns	Batsman	Match	Venue	Season
98	97	C. Hill	Aus v. Eng	Adelaide	1901–02
95	93	F.E. Woolley	Eng v. Aus	Lord's	1921
91	96	C.G. Greenidge	WI v. Pak	Georgetown	1976–77
91	97	C.G. Greenidge	WI v. NZ	Christchurch	1979–80

A NINETY AND A FIFTY[a] IN SAME TEST

1st inns	2nd inns	Batsman	Match	Venue	Season
97	62	J.T. Tyldesley	Eng v. Aus	Melbourne	1903–04
75	95	V.S. Ransford	Aus v. SAf	Melbourne	1910–11
52	92	G.A. Faulkner	SAf v. Aus	Sydney	1910–11
64	97	J.B. Hobbs	Eng v. SAf	Durban	1913–14
72	90	J.M. Taylor	Aus v. Eng	Melbourne	1924–25
67	98	R.H. Catterall	SAf v. Eng	Birmingham	1929
83	95*	F.E. Woolley	Eng v. SAf	Leeds	1929
66	92	R.K. Nunes	WI v. Eng	Kingston	1929–30
93	86	E.H. Hendren	Eng v. SAf	Cape Town	1930–31
75	95	B. Mitchell	SAf v. Aus	Adelaide	1931–32
94	76	L. Hutton	Eng v. Aus	Adelaide	1946–47
99	56	B. Mitchell	SAf v. Eng	Port Elizabeth	1948–49
96	54*	F.B. Smith	NZ v. Eng	Leeds	1949
71	92	R.T. Spooner	Eng v. Ind	Calcutta	1951–52
92	50	J.C. Watkins	SAf v. Aus	Melbourne	1952–53
55	90*	E.D. Weekes	WI v. Eng	Kingston	1953–54
93	64	N.S. Harford (on debut)	NZ v. Pak	Lahore	1955–56

1st inns	2nd inns	Batsman	Match	Venue	Season
75	92	R.B. Simpson	Aus v. WI	Melbourne	1960–61
70	99	E.R. Dexter	Eng v. Aus	Brisbane	1962–63
93	52	E.R. Dexter	Eng v. Aus	Melbourne	1962–63
93	53	S.M. Nurse	WI v. Eng	Nottingham	1966
95	74*	G.S. Sobers	WI v. Ind	Madras	1966–67
93	62*	K.D. Walters	Aus v. Ind	Brisbane	1967–68
76	96	I.M. Chappell	Aus v. WI	Adelaide	1968–69
92	63	A.P.E. Knott	Eng v. Aus	The Oval	1972
53	91	A.I. Kallicharran	WI v. Aus	Port–of–Spain	1972–73
61	92	G. Boycott	Eng v. NZ	Lord's	1973
99	52*	R. Edwards	Aus v. Eng	Lord's	1975
73	92	D.S. Steele	Eng v. Aus	Leeds	1975
95*	69	K.D. Boyce	WI v. Aus	Adelaide	1975–76
50	98	I.V.A. Richards	WI v. Aus	Melbourne	1975–76
90	58	Zaheer Abbas	Pak v. Aus	Melbourne	1976–77
92	64*	K.J. Hughes	Aus v. Ind	Calcutta	1979–80
97	61	Wasim Raja	Pak v. Ind	Delhi	1979–80
92	75	B.M. Laird (on debut)	Aus v. WI	Brisbane	1979–80
99	51	G.A. Gooch	Eng v. Aus	Melbourne	1979–80
60	97	R.L. Dias	SL v. Ind	Madras	1982–83
91	80	M. Amarnath	Ind v. WI	Bridgetown	1982–83
98	70	K.C. Wessels	Aus v. WI	Adelaide	1984–85
78	95	M. Amarnath	Ind v. Eng	Madras	1984–85
96	89	Qasim Omar	Pak v. NZ	Dunedin	1984–85
95	60*	R.L. Dias	SL v. Ind	Colombo	1985–86
94	54	Javed Miandad	Pak v. Ind	Madras	1986–87
81	95*	A.L. Logie	WI v. Eng	Lord's	1988
93	59	R.B. Richardson	WI v. Ind	Bridgetown	1988–89
94	58*	D.C. Boon	Aus v. Eng	Lord's	1989
67	95	Shoaib Mohd	Pak v. Ind	Karachi	1989–90
93	50	S.V. Manjrekar	Ind v. Eng	Manchester	1990
57	96	G.R.J. Matthews	Aus v. SL	Moratuwa	1992–93
80	99	M.A. Atherton	Eng v. Aus	Lord's	1993

a) A fifty represents scores from 50 to 89.

A NINETY AND A DUCK IN THE SAME TEST

1st inns	2nd inns	Batsman	Match	Venue	Season
0	92	G.H.S. Trott	Aus v. Eng	The Oval	1893
0	98	C. Hill	Aus v. Eng	Adelaide	1911–12
0	93	S.J. McCabe	Aus v. Eng	Sydney	1936–37
98	0	J. Hardstaff, Jr	Eng v. WI	Bridgetown	1947–48
0	91	P.B.H. May	Eng v. Aus	Melbourne	1954–55

1st inns	2nd inns	Batsman	Match	Venue	Season
91	0	J.W. Guy	NZ v. Ind	Calcutta	1955–56
93	0	R.A. McLean	SAf v. Eng	Johannesburg	1956–57
0	99	Pankaj Roy	Ind v. Aus	Delhi	1959–60
92	0	R.B. Simpson	Aus v. WI	Brisbane	1960–61
95	0	P.B.H. May	Eng v. Aus	Manchester	1961
93	0	C.G. Borde	Ind v. WI	Kingston	1961–62
0	94	Hanumant Singh	Ind v. Aus	Madras	1964–65
91	0	J.M. Parks	Eng v. WI	Lord's	1966
0	91	A.L. Wadekar	Ind v. Eng	Leeds	1967
95	0	Mansur Pataudi	Ind v. Aus	Bombay	1969–70
99	0	Mushtaq Mohd	Pak v. Eng	Karachi	1972–73
0	95*	R.B. McCosker	Aus v. Eng	Leeds	1975
95	0	G.J. Gilmour	Aus v. WI	Adelaide	1975–76
94	0	G.P. Howarth	NZ v. Eng	The Oval	1978
0	91*	G.A. Gooch	Eng v. NZ	The Oval	1978
0	99*	G. Boycott	Eng v. Aus	Perth	1979–80
94	0	D.B. Vengsarkar	Ind v. WI	St John's	1982–83
0	96	S. Wettimuny	SL v. Aus	Kandy	1982–83
90	0	K.C. Wessels	Aus v. WI	Melbourne	1984–85
0	96	M.W. Gatting	Eng v. Aus	Sydney	1986–87
94	0	K. Srikkanth	Ind v. NZ	Bombay	1988–89
0	96	W.V. Raman	Ind v. NZ	Christchurch	1989–90
0	91*	A.R. Border	Aus v. Ind	Adelaide	1991–92
0	95*	K.C. Wessels	SAf v. Ind	Port Elizabeth	1992–93
96	0	G.W. Flower	Zim v. Ind	Delhi	1992–93

OVERNIGHT NOT OUT ON NINETIES

So far 123 batsmen have gone through 'sleepless nights', remaining not out on nineties at stumps. Appropriately, 100 of them went on to record centuries (11 of them going on to make double centuries), while 23 failed to reach the hundred. England's Arthur Shrewsbury was the first batsman to suffer such a restless night, being 91 not out on the first day of the Lord's Test against Australia in 1886, and went on to reach 164 the next day.

Nine of these batsmen must have needed strong sedatives at night, being 99 not out at stumps! English great Jack Hobbs was the first one in this 'Shaky Bed Club' and Pakistan's Mudassar Nazar is the only player to twice spend the night on 99.

Batsmen in the nineties overnight (O/N) who went on to complete a century are listed opposite:

O/N	Batsman	Final score	Match	Venue	Season
99	J.B. Hobbs	119	Eng v. Aus	Adelaide	1924–25
	W.R. Hammond	120	Eng v. SAf	Durban	1938–39
	G.E. Gomez	101	WI v. Ind	Delhi	1948–49
	G.M. Turner	110	NZ v. Pak	Dacca	1969–70
	Mudassar Nazar	126	Pak v. Ind	Bangalore	1979–80
	G.S. Chappell	114	Aus v. Eng	Melbourne	1979–80
	Mudassar Nazar	152	Pak v. Ind	Lahore	1982–83
	A.J. Lamb	113	Eng v. WI	Lord's	1988
	Javed Miandad	153*	Pak v. Eng	Birmingham	1992
	G.A. Hick	178	Eng v. Ind	Bombay	1992–93
98	A.D. Nourse	231	SAf v. Aus	Johannesburg	1935–36
	P.B.H. May	104	Eng v. Aus	Sydney	1954–55
	C.C. McDonald	133	Aus v. Eng	Melbourne	1958–59
	P.J.P. Burge	103	Aus v. Eng	Sydney	1962–63
	Asif Iqbal	104*	Pak v. Eng	Birmingham	1971
	R.C. Fredericks	150	WI v. Eng	Birmingham	1973
	M. Azharuddin	122	Ind v. Eng	Kanpur	1984–85
	A.R. Border	163	Aus v. Ind	Melbourne	1985–86
	D.B. Vengsarkar	166	Ind v. SL	Cuttack	1986–87
	Basit Ali	103	Pak v. NZ	Christchurch	1993–94
97	P.F. Warner	132*	Eng v. SAf	Johannesburg	1898–99
	D.G. Bradman	167	Aus v. SAf	Melbourne	1931–32
	D.N. Sardesai	200*	Ind v. NZ	Bombay	1964–65
	R. Illingworth	113	Eng v. WI	Lord's	1969
	C.T. Radley	158	Eng v. NZ	Auckland	1977–78
	G.S. Chappell	124	Aus v. WI	Brisbane	1979–80
	G.S. Chappell	235	Aus v. Pak	Faisalabad	1979–80
	I.V.A. Richards	109	WI v. Ind	Georgetown	1982–83
96	A. Melville	117	SAf v. Eng	Lord's	1947
	K.R. Miller	145*	Aus v. Eng	Sydney	1950–51
	I.R. Redpath	132	Aus v. WI	Sydney	1968–69
	S.M. Gavaskar	111	Ind v. Pak	Karachi	1978–79
	A.J. Lamb	107	Eng v. Ind	The Oval	1982
	Javed Miandad	114	Pak v. WI	Georgetown	1987–88
	M.A. Taylor	136	Aus v. Eng	Leeds	1989
95	V.T. Trumper	113	Aus v. Eng	Sydney	1911–12
	M. Leyland	109	Eng v. Aus	Lord's	1934
	V.S. Hazare	155	Ind v. Eng	Bombay	1951–52
	C.L. Walcott	108	WI v. Aus	Kingston	1954–55
	G.S. Sobers	142*	WI v. Ind	Bombay	1958–59

O/N	Batsman	Final score	Match	Venue	Season
	M.C. Cowdrey	104	Eng v. Aus	Birmingham	1968
	R.W. Marsh	110*	Aus v. Eng	Melbourne	1976–77
	Qasim Omar	206	Pak v. SL	Faisalabad	1985–86
	Javed Miandad	211	Pak v. Aus	Karachi	1988–89
	I.V.A. Richards	146	WI v. Aus	Perth	1988–89
	G.A. Gooch	154	Eng v. NZ	Birmingham	1990
	R.J. Shastri	206	Ind v. Aus	Sydney	1991–92
94	W.W. Armstrong	159*	Aus v. SAf	Johannesburg	1902–03
	F.E. Woolley	123	Eng v. Aus	Sydney	1924–25
	P.R. Umrigar	108	Ind v. Pak	Peshawar	1954–55
	Saeed Ahmed	121	Pak v. Ind	Bombay	1960–61
	M.C. Cowdrey	113	Eng v. Aus	Melbourne	1962–63
	L.G. Rowe	214	WI v. NZ	Kingston	1971–72
	A.W. Greig	103	Eng v. Ind	Calcutta	1976–77
	Kapil Dev	126*	Ind v. WI	Delhi	1978–79
	G.R. Viswanath	179	Ind v. WI	Kanpur	1978–79
	Muddassar Nazar	119	Pak v. Ind	Karachi	1982–83
	S.M. Gavaskar	166*	Ind v. Aus	Adelaide	1985–86
	M.A. Atherton	105	Eng v. Aus	Sydney	1990–91
	A.J. Stewart	190	Eng v. Pak	Birmingham	1992
	R.B. Richardson	109	WI v. Aus	Sydney	1992–93
	M.A. Taylor	142*	Aus v. NZ	Perth	1993–94
93	M. Leyland	153	Eng v. Aus	Manchester	1934
	B. Mitchell	120	SAf v. Eng	Cape Town	1948–49
	R.A. McLean	101	SAf v. NZ	Durban	1953–54
	L. Hutton	205	Eng v. WI	Kingston	1953–54
	N.C. O'Neill	113	Aus v. Ind	Calcutta	1959–60
	K.F. Barrington	121	Eng v. WI	Port–of–Spain	1959–60
	G. Boycott	116	Eng v. WI	Georgetown	1967–68
	P.A. de Silva	122	SL v. Pak	Faisalabad	1985–86
	S.V. Manjrekar	108	Ind v. WI	Bridgetown	1988–89
	G.A. Gooch	135	Eng v. Pak	Leeds	1992
	S.A. Thomson	120*	NZ v. Pak	Christchurch	1993–94
92	E.H. Hendren	142	Eng v. SAf	The Oval	1924
	D.G. Bradman	152	Aus v. WI	Melbourne	1930–31
	C.J. Barnett	129	Eng v. Aus	Adelaide	1936–37
	B. Mitchell	120	SAf v. Eng	The Oval	1947
	E.C. Weekes	207	WI v. Ind	Port–of–Spain	1952–53
	O.G. Smith	104	WI v. Aus	Kingston	1954–55
	Majid Khan	158	Pak v. Aus	Melbourne	1972–73
	D.L. Amiss	174	Eng v. WI	Port–of–Spain	1973–74

O/N	Batsman	Final score	Match	Venue	Season
92	S.M. Gavaskar	166	Ind v. Pak	Madras	1979–80
	D.L. Haynes	184	WI v. Eng	Lord's	1980
	Mudassar Nazar	231	Pak v. Ind	Hyderabad (Pak)	1982–83
	Salim Malik	116	Pak v. Eng	Faisalabad	1983–84
	A.R. Border	196	Aus v. Eng	Lord's	1985
91	A. Shrewsbury	164	Eng v. Aus	Lord's	1886
	F.M.M. Worrell	197*	WI v. Eng	Bridgetown	1959–60
	P.G.Z. Harris	101	NZ v. SAf	Cape Town	1961–62
	P. Willey	102*	Eng v. WI	St John's	1980–81
	J.G. Wright	141	NZ v. Aus	Christchurch	1981–82
	K.R. Rutherford	107*	NZ v. Eng	Wellington	1987–88
	D.C. Boon	107	Aus v. Ind	Perth	1991–92
	R.A. Smith	128	Eng v. SL	Colombo	1993–94
90	C.A.G. Russell	111	Eng v. SAf	Durban	1922–23
	C.C. McDonald	110	Aus v. WI	Port–of–Spain	1954–55
	M.C. Cowdrey	107	Eng v. Ind	Calcutta	1963–64
	R. Edwards	170*	Aus v. Eng	Nottingham	1972
	S.M. Gavaskar	156	Ind v. WI	Port–of–Spain	1975–76
	Shoaib Mohammad	203*	Pak v. Ind	Lahore	1989–90

Note: Greg Chappell in 1979–80 and Mudassar Nazar in 1982–83 remained unbeaten in their nineties three times each and completed their centuries the following day. Alec Russell (90 to 111) was playing his final Test innings.

Batsmen in their nineties O/N who did not complete their century are listed below:

O/N	Batsman	Final score	Match	Venue	Season
97	J.T. Tyldesley	97	Eng v. Aus	Melbourne	1903–04
	A.L. Wadekar	99	Ind v. Aus	Melbourne	1967–68
	G. Boycott	99	Eng v. WI	Port–of–Spain	1973–74
96	T.W. Graveny	97	Eng v. Pak	Birmingham	1962
95	G.S. Sobers	95	WI v. Ind	Madras	1966–67
	R.B. McCosker	95*	Aus v. Eng	Leeds	1975
	K.D. Boyce	95*	WI v. Aus	Adelaide	1975–76
94	Wasim Raja	97	Pak v. Ind	Delhi	1979–80

O/N	Batsman	Final score	Match	Venue	Season
93	M.C. Cowdrey	93*	Eng v. Aus	The Oval	1964
	J.H. Edrich	96	Eng v. Ind	Lord's	1974
	J.R. Ratnayeke	93	SL v. Ind	Kanpur	1986–87
92	W. Rhodes	92	Eng v. Aus	Manchester	1912
	H. Sutcliffe	99	Eng v. SAf	Cape Town	1927–28
	C.L. McCool	95	Aus v. Eng	Brisbane	1946–47
	Javed Miandad	92	Pak v. SL	Karachi	1981–82
91	Shafqat Rana	95	Pak v. NZ	Lahore	1969–70
	G. Boycott	93	Eng v. WI	Port–of–Spain	1973–74
	J.H. Edrich	96	Eng v. Aus	The Oval	1975
	G.N. Yallop	98	Aus v. SL	Kandy	1982–83
90	C. Washbrook	98	Eng v. Aus	Leeds	1956
	R.M. Cowper	99	Aus v. Eng	Melbourne	1965–66
	G. Boycott	90	Eng v. WI	Bridgetown	1967–68
	S.R. Tendulkar	96	Ind v. SL	Bangalore	1993–94

Note: Geoff Boycott was in the nineties at stumps on four occasions, but managed to score a century only once. In the series against the West Indies in 1973–74, he was twice in the nineties overnight but failed to reach the century both times. However, in the Port–of–Spain Test in the same series (when he progressed from 97 to 99 in the first innings), he scored 112 in the second. Rick McCosker could not bat on the last day because the pitch was vandalised; Keith Boyce was left partnerless because the last-man-in, Lance Gibbs, was bowled; and heavy rains completely washed out last day's play leaving Colin Cowdrey stranded on 93.

INDIVIDUAL NINETIES IN TEST CRICKET

Batsman	How out		Opp.	Venue	Season
Australia					
A.C. Bannerman	c W. Bates b F. Morley	94	Eng	Sydney	1882–83
	c W.G. Grace b J. Briggs	91	Eng	Sydney	1891–92
G.H.S. Trott	c W.W. Read b W.H. Lockwood	92	Eng	The Oval	1893
	c & b W. Brockwell	95	Eng	Melbourne	1894–95
C. Hill	b J.T. Hearne	96	Eng	Sydney	1897–98
	c A.D. Jones b S.F. Barnes	99	Eng	Melbourne	1901–02
	c J.T. Tyldesley b L.C. Braund	98	Eng	Adelaide	1901–02
	b G.L. Jessop	97	Eng	Adelaide	1901–02
	NOT OUT	91	SAf	Cape Town	1902–03

Batsman	How out		Opp.	Venue	Season
C. Hill	c J.W. Hitch b S.F. Barnes	98	Eng	Adelaide	1911–12
V.S. Ransford	b G.A. Faulkner	95	SAf	Melbourne	1910–11
W. Bardsley	c & b J.H. Sinclair	94	SAf	Sydney	1910–11
R.B. Minnett (on debut)	c F.R. Foster b S.F. Barnes	90	Eng	Sydney	1911–12
W.W. Armstrong	b F.R. Foster	90	Eng	Melbourne	1911–12
C.G. Macartney	c E.J. Smith b F.R. Foster	99	Eng	Lord's	1912
J.M. Gregory	c H. Strudwick b P.G.H. Fender	93	Eng	Sydney	1920–21
T.J.E. Andrews	b V.W.C. Jupp	92	Eng	Leeds	1921
	lbw b C.H. Parkin	94	Eng	The Oval	1921
A.J. Richardson (on debut)	c & b A.P. Freeman	98	Eng	Sydney	1924–25
J.M. Taylor	b M.W. Tate	90	Eng	Melbourne	1924–25
S.J. McCabe	c & b L.N. Constantine	90	WI	Adelaide	1930–31
	lbw b W. Voce	93	Eng	Sydney	1936–37
W.H. Ponsford	NOT OUT	92	WI	Adelaide	1930–31
A.G. Chipperfield (on debut)	c L.E.G. Ames b K. Farnes	99	Eng	Nottingham	1934
C. McCool	lbw b D.V.P. Wright	95	Eng	Brisbane	1946–47
D. Tallon	c & b D.V.P. Wright	92	Eng	Melbourne	1946–47
W.A. Brown	Run out	99	Ind	Melbourne	1947–48
S.J.E. Loxton	b N.W.D. Yardley	93	Eng	Leeds	1948
K.R. Miller	b D.V.P. Wright	99	Eng	Adelaide	1950–51
A.L. Hassett	c L. Hutton b F.R. Brown	92	Eng	Melbourne	1950–51
A.R. Morris	Run out	99	SAf	Melbourne	1952–53
R.N. Harvey	NOT OUT	92	Eng	Sydney	1954–55
	b Fazal Mahmood	96	Pak	Dacca	1959–60
R.G. Archer	b F.M.M. Worrell	98	WI	Bridgetown	1954–55
R. Benaud	c T.G. Evans b F.S. Trueman	97	Eng	Lord's	1956
	c D.B. Pithey b P.M. Pollock	90	SAf	Sydney	1963–64
C.C. McDonald	c J.H.B. White b E.R.H. Fuller	99	SAf	Cape Town	1957–58
	lbw G.S. Sobers	91	WI	Melbourne	1960–61

Batsman	How out		Opp.	Venue	Season
R.B. Simpson	b S. Ramadhim	92	WI	Brisbane	1960–61
	b L.R. Gibbs	92	WI	Melbourne	1960–61
	b F.J. Titmus	91	Eng	Sydney	1962–63
	lbw b P.H.J. Trimborn	94	SAf	Durban	1966–67
W.M. Lawry	c D.S. Sheppard b F.J. Titmus	98	Eng	Brisbane	1962–63
	c F.S. Trueman b E.R. Dexter	94	Eng	The Oval	1964
	c D. Lindsay b T.L. Goddard	98	SAf	J'burg	1966–67
I.R. Redpath	b J.T. Partridge	97	SAf	Melbourne	1963–64
(on debut)	b R. Illingworth	92	Eng	Leeds	1968
	c H.J. Howarth b B.E. Congdon	93	NZ	Wellington	1973–74
B.K. Shepherd	c D.B. Pithey b E.J. Barlow	96	SAf	Melbourne	1963–64
P.J. Burge	c G.G. Halse b P.M. Pollock	91	SAf	Adelaide	1963–64
B.C. Booth	c & b J.S.E. Price	98	Eng	Manchester	1964
R.M. Cowper	c F.J. Titmus b I.J. Jones	99	Eng	Melbourne	1965–66
	c F.M. Engineer b S. Abid Ali	92	Ind	Adelaide	1967–68
K.D. Walters	c A.L. Wadekar b U.N. Kulkarni	93	Ind	Brisbane	1967–68
	NOT OUT	94	Ind	Sydney	1967–68
	b D.R. O'Sullivan	94	NZ	Adelaide	1973–74
I.M. Chappell	lbw b C.C. Griffith	96	WI	Adelaide	1968–69
	c A.L. Wadekar b B.S. Bedi	99	Ind	Calcutta	1969–70
	c R. Fredericks b E. Willett	97	WI	Port-of-Sp.	1972–73
	c A.W. Grieg b R.G.D. Willis	90	Eng	Brisbane	1974–75
R.W. Marsh	NOT OUT	92	Eng	Melbourne	1970–71
	c A.P.E. Knott b A.W. Greig	91	Eng	Manchester	1972
	hit wicket b U. Dowe	97	WI	Kingston	1972–73
	c J.V. Coney b R.J. Hadlee	91	NZ	Perth	1980–81
R. Edwards	lbw b R.A. Woolmer	99	Eng	Lord's	1975
R. McCosker	NOT OUT	95	Eng	Leeds	1975
G.Gilmour	c M.H. Holding b L.R. Gibbs	95	WI	Adelaide	1975–76
G.M. Wood	c S.F. Bacchus b R.R. Jumadeen	90	WI	Kingston	1977–78
P.M. Toohey	st D.A. Murray b R.R. Jumadeen	97	WI	Kingston	1977–78
W.H. Darling	c I.T. Botham b G. Miller	91	Eng	Sydney	1978–79
K.J. Hughes	lbw b Kapil Dev	92	Ind	Calcutta	1979–80
	c J.M. Brearly b D.L. Underwood	99	Eng	Perth	1979–80
	lbw b Azeem Hafeez	94	Pak	Melbourne	1983–84

Batsman	How out		Opp.	Venue	Season
B.M. Laird (on debut)	c D.L. Murray b J. Garner	92	WI	Brisbane	1979–80
G.S. Chappell	NOT OUT	98	Eng	Sydney	1979–80
J.M. Weiner	lbw b Iqbal Qasim	93	Pak	Lahore	1979–80
G.N. Yallop	lbw b A.L.F. de Mel	98	SL	Kandy	1982–83
A.R. Border	NOT OUT	98	WI	Port-of-Sp.	1983–84
	c P.J.L. Dujon b E.A.E. Baptiste	98	WI	St John's	1983–84
	NOT OUT	91	Ind	Adelaide	1991–92
K.C. Wessels[a]	b M.D. Marshall	98	WI	Adelaide	1984–85
	c P.J.L. Dujon b M.D. Marshall	90	WI	Melbourne	1984–85
W.B. Phillips	c A.J. Lamb b I.T. Botham	91	Eng	Leeds	1985
G.M. Ritchie	lbw b I.T. Botham	94	Eng	Lord's	1985
	b G.B. Troupe	92	NZ	Wellington	1985–86
G.R. Marsh	c S.M. Gavaskar b R.J. Shastri	92	Ind	Sydney	1985–86
	c C.L. Hooper b B.P. Patterson	94	WI	Georgetown	1990–91
D.M. Jones	c C.J. Richards b G.R. Dilley	93	Eng	Adelaide	1986–87
	lbw b D.K. Morrison	99	NZ	Perth	1989–90
P.R. Sleep	lbw b R.J. Hadlee	90	NZ	Melbourne	1987–88
S.R. Waugh	c D.L. Haynes b M.D. Marshall	90	WI	Brisbane	1988–89
	c P.J.L. Dujon b C.E.L. Ambrose	91	WI	Perth	1988–89
	c T.S. Curtis b N.A. Fraser	92	Eng	Manchester	1989
D.C. Boon	c G.A. Gooch b G.R. Dilley	94	Eng	Lord's	1989
	NOT OUT	94	Eng	Melbourne	1990–91
	c M.A. Atherton b G.A. Gooch	97	Eng	Sydney	1990–91
	c M.W. Gatting b P. De Freitas	93	Eng	Manchester	1993
	c D.J. Richardson b F. de Villiers	96	SAf	Cape Town	1993–94
M.A. Taylor	c D.B. Vengsarkar b S.L.V. Raju	94	Ind	Brisbane	1991–92
G.R.J. Matthews	b C.P.H. Ramanayake	96	SL	Moratuwa	1992–93
M.E. Waugh	b P.C.R. Tufnell	99	Eng	Lord's	1993
M.J. Slater	c T.E. Bain b D.N. Patel	99	NZ	Perth	1993–94
	b A.A. Donald	92	SAf	Sydney	1993–94
	lbw b A.A. Donald	95	SAf	Durban	1993–94

[a] Also two nineties for South Africa

Batsman	How out		Opp.	Venue	Season
England					
W.H. Scotton	c H.J.H. Scott b G. Giffen	90	Aus	The Oval	1884
W.W. Read	c S.P. Jones b F.R. Spofforth	94	Aus	The Oval	1886
F.S. Jackson (on debut)	c J. McC. Blackham b C. Turner	91	Aus	Lord's	1893
A. Ward	b G.H.S. Trott	93	Aus	Melbourne	1894–95
R. Abel	b C.J. Eady	94	Aus	Lord's	1896
K.S. Ranjitsinhji	NOT OUT	93	Aus	Nottingham	1899
T.W. Hayward	Run out	90	Aus	Adelaide	1901–02
	st J.J. Kelly b J.V. Saunders	91	Aus	Sydney	1903–04
A.C. MacLaren	c R.A. Duff b J.V. Saunders	92	Aus	Sydney	1901–02
J.T. Tyldesley	c H. Trumble b W.P. Howell	97	Aus	Melbourne	1903–04
G.L. Jessop	c G.A. Faulkner b A.E.E. Vogler	93	SAf	Lord's	1907
J.B. Hobbs	NOT OUT	93	SAf	J'burg	1909–10
	c T.A. Ward b C.D. Dixon	92	SAf	J'burg	1913–14
	b J.M. Blackenberg	97	SAf	Durban	1913–14
W. Rhodes	b W.J. Whitty	92	Aus	Manchester	1912
F.E. Woolley	st H. Carter b A.A. Mailey	95	Aus	Lord's	1921
	c H.L. Hendry b A.A. Mailey	93	Aus	Lord's	1921
	NOT OUT	95	SAf	Leeds	1929
C.A.G. Russell	c A.E. Hall b E.P. Nupen	96	SAf	J'burg	1922–23
E.H. Hendren	c J.M. Taylor b J.M. Gregory	92	Aus	Adelaide	1924–25
	c P.M. Hornibrook b A. Fairfax	95	Aus	Melbourne	1928–29
	b X. Balaskas	93	SAf	Cape Town	1930–31
H. Sutcliffe	b A.J. Richardson	94	Aus	Leeds	1926
	b G.F. Bissett	99	SAf	Cape Town	1927–28
R.E.S. Wyatt	c H. Promnitz b G.F. Bissett	91	SAf	Cape Town	1927–28
W.R. Hammond	b C.L. Vincent	90	SAf	Durban	1927–28
D.R. Jardine	c W.M. Woodfull b R.Oxenham	98	Aus	Adelaide	1928–29
M. Leyland	lbw b A.E. Hall	91	SAf	J'burg	1930–31
H. Larwood	c H. Ironmonger b P.K. Lee	98	Aus	Sydney	1932–33

Batsman	How out		Opp.	Venue	Season
J. Hardstaff Jr	c & b L. Amarsingh	94	Ind	Manchester	1936
	b L.N. Constantine	94	WI	The Oval	1939
	b E.A.V. Williams	98	WI	Bridgetown	1947–48
E. Paynter	lbw b W.J. O'Reilly	99	Aus	Lord's	1938
P.A. Gibb (on debut)	c A. Melville b B. Mitchell	93	SAf	J'burg	1938–39
B.H. Valentine	c W.W. Wade b N. Gordon	97	SAf	J'burg	1938–39
L. Hutton	b B. Mitchell	92	SAf	J'burg	1938–39
	lbw b C. McCool	94	Aus	Adelaide	1946–47
	NOT OUT	98	SAf	Manchester	1951
N.W.D. Yardley	c L. Tuckett b O.C. Dawson	99	SAf	Nottingham	1947
C. Washbrook	c E.A.B. Rowan b C. McCarthy	97	SAf	J'burg	1948–49
	lbw b R. Benaud	98	Aus	Leeds	1956
T.E. Bailey	c B. Sutcliffe b G.A. Rabone	93	NZ	Lord's	1949
	b N.B.F. Mann	95	SAf	Leeds	1951
R.T. Simpson	Run out	94	WI	Nottingham	1950
R.T. Spooner	b V. Mankad	92	Ind	Calcutta	1951–52
D.C.S. Compton	lbw b J.B. Stollmeyer	93	WI	Bridgetown	1953–54
	c Imtiaz Ahmed b Shujauddin	93	Pak	Manchester	1954
	c A.K. Davidson b R.G. Archer	94	Aus	The Oval	1956
T.W. Graveny	c & b C.L. Walcott	92	WI	Port-of-Sp.	1953–54
	c I. Butt b Mahmood Hussain	97	Pak	Birmingham	1962
	c D.W. Allan b W.W. Hall	96	WI	Lord's	1966
	b A.N. Connolly	96	Aus	Birmingham	1968
P.B.H. May	b W.A. Johnston	91	Aus	Melbourne	1954–55
	lbw b H.J. Tayfield	97	SAf	Leeds	1955
	b J.W. Burke	92	Aus	Sydney	1958–59
	c R.B. Simpson b A.K. Davidson	95	Aus	Manchester	1961
R. Subba Row	c N.S. Tamhane b R.B. Desai	94	Ind	The Oval	1959
	lbw b N.A.T. Adcock	90	SAf	Lord's	1960
M.J.K. Smith	b R.B. Desai	98	Ind	The Oval	1959
	c F.C.M. Alexander b C.C. Hunte	96	WI	Port-of-Sp.	1959–60
	c J.H.B. Waite b G.M. Griffin	99	SAf	Lord's	1960
	Run out	99	Pak	Lahore	1961–62
M.C. Cowdrey	c F.C.M. Alexander b R. Scarlett	97	WI	Kingston	1959–60
	c A.T.W. Grout b G.D. McKenzie	93	Aus	Leeds	1961

Batsman	How out		Opp.	Venue	Season
M.C. Cowdrey	NOT OUT	93	Aus	The Oval	1964
	c J.L. Hendricks b C.C. Griffin	96	WI	Nottingham	1966
E.R. Dexter	b G.D. McKenzie	99	Aus	Brisbane	1962–63
	c R.B. Simpson b R. Benaud	93	Aus	Melbourne	1962–63
K.F. Barrington	c A.T.W. Grout b G.D. McKenzie	94	Aus	Sydney	1962–63
	c J.H.B. Waite b E.J. Barlow	93	SAf	J'burg	1963–64
	Run out	91	SAf	Lord's	1965
	Run out	93	Ind	Leeds	1967
	b B.S. Chandrasekhar	97	Ind	Lord's	1967
R.W. Barber	b M.A. Seymour	97	SAf	J'burg	1963–64
C. Milburn (on debut)	b L.R. Gibbs	94	WI	Manchester	1966
J.M. Parks	lbw b M.C. Carew	91	WI	Lord's	1966
J.H. Edrich	c R.B. Kanhai b G.S. Sobers	96	WI	Kingston	1967–68
	lbw b B.S. Bedi	96	Ind	Lord's	1974
	b D.K. Lillee	96	Aus	The Oval	1975
G. Boycott	lbw b G.S. Sobers	90	WI	Bridgetown	1967–68
	c & b H.J. Howarth	92	NZ	Lord's	1973
	c D.L. Murray b B.D. Julien	97	WI	The Oval	1973
	c R.C. Fredericks b L.R. Gibbs	93	WI	Port-of-Sp.	1973–74
	c D.L. Murray b B.D. Julien	99	WI	Port-of-Sp.	1973–74
	NOT OUT	99	Aus	Perth	1979–80
A.P.E. Knott	NOT OUT	96	Pak	Karachi	1968–69
	b R.S. Cunis	96	NZ	Auckland	1970–71
	c & b E.D. Solkar	90	Ind	The Oval	1971
	c R.W. Marsh b D.K. Lillee	92	Aus	The Oval	1972
B.N. Luckhurst	c G.S. Chappell b I.M. Chappell	96	Aus	Nottingham	1972
B. Wood (on debut)	lbw b R.A.L. Massie	90	Aus	The Oval	1972
K.W.R. Fletcher	NOT OUT	97	Ind	Madras	1972–73
D.L. Amiss	c Sarfraz Nawaz b Intikhab Alam	99	Pak	Karachi	1972–73
	c I.M. Chappell b A.A. Mallett	90	Aus	Melbourne	1974–75
A.W. Greig	c I.M. Chappell b M.H.N. Walker	96	Aus	Lord's	1975
	c K.J. O'Keeffe b L.S. Pascoe	91	Aus	Lord's	1977
D.S. Steele	c G.S. Chappell b G.J. Gilmour	92	Aus	Leeds	1975
J.M. Brearley	st S. Kirmani b E. Prasanna	91	Ind	Bombay	1976–77

Batsman	How out		Opp.	Venue	Season
G. Miller	NOT OUT	98	Pak	Lahore	1977–78
	c D.B. Vengsarkar b D.R. Doshi	98	Ind	Manchester	1982
G.A. Gooch	NOT OUT	91	NZ	The Oval	1978
	Run out	99	Aus	Melbourne	1979–80
	b Mudassar Nazar	93	Pak	Karachi	1987–88
R.W. Taylor	c K.J. Wright b R.M. Hogg	97	Aus	Adelaide	1978–79
D.I. Gower	NOT OUT	98	Aus	Sydney	1979–80
	c P.J.L. Dujon b M.D. Marshall	90	WI	St John's	1985–86
D.W. Randall	st S.M.H. Kirmani b R.J. Shastri	95	Ind	The Oval	1982
E.E. Hemmings	c R.W. Marsh b B. Yardley	95	Aus	Sydney	1982–83
C.L. Smith	c I.D.S. Smith b R.J. Hadlee	91	NZ	Auckland	1983–84
R.T. Robinson	lbw b Kapil Dev	96	Ind	Kanpur	1984–85
C.W.J. Athey	b B.A. Reid	96	Aus	Perth	1986–87
M.W. Gatting	c & b S.R. Waugh	96	Aus	Sydney	1986–87
D.J. Capel	b Abdul Qadir	98	Pak	Karachi	1987–88
M.D. Moxon	c J.J. Crowe b J.G. Bracewell	99	NZ	Auckland	1987–88
R.C. Russell (on debut)	c M. Samarasekera b G. Labrooy	94	SL	Lord's	1988
R.A. Smith	b T.M. Alderman	96	Aus	Lord's	1989
	c M.J. Greatbach b C. Pringle	96	NZ	Christchurch	1991–92
A.J. Stewart	lbw b T.M. Alderman	91	Aus	Sydney	1990–91
A.J. Lamb	c A.R. Border b C.J. McDermott	91	Aus	Perth	1990–91
	b D.N. Patel	93	NZ	Christchurch	1991–92
M.A. Atherton	Run out	99	Aus	Lord's	1993
G.A. Hick	c(sub) b K.C.G. Benjamin	96	WI	Kingston	1993–94
South Africa					
L.J. Tancred (on debut)	c R.A. Duff b V.T. Trumper	97	Aus	J'burg	1902–03
C.B. Llewellyn	b V.T. Trumper	90	Aus	J'burg	1902–03
A.W. Nourse	NOT OUT	93	Eng	J'burg	1905–06
	NOT OUT	92	Aus	Melbourne	1910–11
G.A. Faulkner	c F.E. Woolley b G.J. Thompson	99	Eng	Cape Town	1909–10

Batsman	How out		Opp.	Venue	Season
G.A. Faulkner	b A. Cotter	92	Aus	Sydney	1910–11
H.W. Taylor	c C. Kelleway b G.R. Hazlitt	93	Aus	Lord's	1912
	lbw b S.F. Barnes	93	Eng	Durban	1913–14
	c F.E. Woolley b G.G. Macauley	91	Eng	Durban	1922–23
R.H. Catterall	c(sub) b M.W. Tate	95	Eng	The Oval	1924
	c J.C. White b P.G.H. Fender	98	Eng	Birmingham	1929
H.G. Deane	c F.E. Woolley b R.E.S. Wyatt	93	Eng	The Oval	1929
B. Mitchell	c W.J. O'Reilly b C.V. Grimmett	95	Aus	Adelaide	1931–32
	c S.C. Griffith b A.V. Bedser	99	Eng	Port Eliz.	1948–49
M.B. Cameron	b M.S. Nichols	90	Eng	Lord's	1935
A.D. Nourse	c J.H. Fingelton b W.J. O'Reilly	91	Aus	Durban	1935–36
	b R. Howarth	97	Eng	The Oval	1947
P.G.V. van der Bijl	c E. Paynter b D.V.P. Wright	97	Eng	Durban	1938–39
K.G. Viljoen	c D.C.S. Compton b W.J. Edrich	93	Eng	Manchester	1947
P.N.F. Mansell (on debut)	c R. Tattersall b M.J. Hilton	90	Eng	Leeds	1951
K.J. Funston	c & b R. Benaud	92	Aus	Adelaide	1952–53
J.C. Watkins	b R.G. Archer	92	Aus	Melbourne	1952–53
W.R. Endean	c B. Sutcliffe b J.R. Reid	93	NZ	J'burg	1953–54
R.A. McLean	Run out	93	Eng	J'burg	1956–57
T.L. Goddard	b I. Meckiff	90	Aus	J'burg	1957–58
	c M.C. Cowdrey b J.B. Statham	99	Eng	The Oval	1960
	c A.T.W. Grout b T.R. Veivers	93	Aus	Sydney	1963–64
S. O'Linn	c M.C. Cowdrey b A.E. Moss	98	Eng	Nottingham	1960
E.J. Barlow	c J.T. Ward b F.J. Cameron	92	NZ	Wellington	1963–64
	c & b T.W. Cartwright	96	Eng	J'burg	1964–65
A.J. Pithey	c T.W. Cartwright b F.J. Titmus	95	Eng	J'burg	1964–65
R.G. Pollock	b R.M. Cowper	90	Aus	J'burg	1966–67
J.N. Rhodes	lbw b A.R. Kumble	91	Ind	J'burg	1992–93
B.M. McMillan	c S.V. Manjrekar b J. Srinath	98	Ind	J'burg	1992–93
K.C. Wessels[a]	NOT OUT	95	Ind	Port Eliz.	1992–93
	c P.Dissanayake b M. Muralidharan	92	SL	Colombo	1993–94

Batsman	How out		Opp.	Venue	Season
A.C. Hudson	c A.P. Gurusinha b P.K. Wijetunge	90	SL	Moratuwa	1993–94
	lbw b S.R. Waugh	90	Aus	Adelaide	1993–94

[a] Also two nineties for Australia

West Indies

Batsman	How out		Opp.	Venue	Season
R.K. Nunes	b W.E. Astill	92	Eng	Kingston	1929–30
J.E.D. Sealy	b R.E.S. Wyatt	92	Eng	Port-of-Sp.	1934–35
	b G.A.E. Paine	91	Eng	Kingston	1934–35
L.N. Constantine	c E.H. Hendren b J. Smith	90	Eng	Port-of-Sp.	1934–35
G.A. Headley	lbw b J. Smith	93	Eng	Port-of-Sp.	1934–35
V.H. Stollmeyer (in only Test innings)	st A. Wood b T.W. Goddard	96	Eng	The Oval	1939
R.J. Christiani (on debut)	lbw b K. Cranston	99	Eng	Bridgetown	1947–48
F.M.M. Worrell (on debut)	c T.G. Evans b K. Cranston	97	Eng	Port-of-Sp.	1947–48
	NOT OUT	98	Ind	Kingston	1961–62
E.D. Weekes	Run out	90	Ind	Madras	1948–49
	NOT OUT	90	Eng	Kingston	1953–54
	b G.A.R. Lock	94	Eng	Georgetown	1953–54
	c T.G. Evans b T.E. Bailey	90	Eng	Lord's	1957
A.F. Rae	c V. Mankad b D.G. Phadkar	97	Ind	Bombay	1948–49
	b T.B. Burtt	99	NZ	Auckland	1951–52
C.L. Walcott	lbw b D.G. Phadkar	98	Ind	Bridgetown	1952–53
	c T.G. Evans b J.C. Laker	90	Eng	Birmingham	1957
J.K. Holt (on debut)	lbw b J.B. Statham	94	Eng	Kingston	1953–54
R.B. Kanhai	c W. Mathias b Mahmood Hussain	96	Pak	Port-of-Sp.	1957–58
	Run out	99	Ind	Madras	1958–59
	Run out	90	Eng	Manchester	1963
	b G.A.R. Lock	92	Eng	Leeds	1963
	c Mansur Ali Khan b R.F. Surti	90	Ind	Calcutta	1966–67
	c J.W. Gleeson b A.A. Mallett	94	Aus	Brisbane	1968–69
C.C. Hunte	lbw b H.R. Adhikari	92	Ind	Delhi	1958–59
G.S. Sobers	b A.E. Moss	92	Eng	Port-of-Sp.	1959–60
	c D.L. Underwood b K. Higgs	94	Eng	Nottingham	1966
	c F. Engineer b B. Chandrasekhar	95	Ind	Madras	1966–67
	NOT OUT	95	Eng	Georgetown	1967–68

Batsman	How out		Opp.	Venue	Season
G.S. Sobers	c P. Krishnamurthy b E.D. Solkar	93	Ind	Kingston	1970–71
J. Solomon	c R.B. Desai b S.A. Durani	96	Ind	Bridgetown	1961–62
S.M. Nurse	c R. Illingworth b J.A. Snow	93	Eng	Nottingham	1966
	c G.M. Turner b V. Pollard	95	NZ	Auckland	1968–69
M.C. Carew	c I.M. Chappell b A.N. Connolly	90	Aus	Adelaide	1968–69
	c G.M. Turner b V. Pollard	91	NZ	Christchurch	1968–69
B.F. Butcher	c A.P.E. Knott b D.L. Underwood	91	Eng	Leeds	1969
M.L.C. Foster	b S. Abid Ali	99	Ind	Port-of-Sp.	1970–71
C.A. Davis	c G.M. Turner b H.J. Howarth	90	NZ	Port-of-Sp.	1971–72
R.C. Fredericks	lbw b J.R. Hammond	98	Aus	Bridgetown	1972–73
	b C.M. Old	94	Eng	Kingston	1973–74
	b A.W. Greig	98	Eng	Georgetown	1973–74
D.L. Murray	c I.R. Redpath b T.R. Jenner	90	Aus	Bridgetown	1972–73
	c B.P. Patel b K. Ghavri	91	Ind	Bombay	1974–75
A.I. Kallicharran	c R.W. Marsh b M.H.N. Walker	91	Aus	Port-of-Sp.	1972–73
	c M.H. Denness b C.M. Old	93	Eng	Kingston	1973–74
	c G.R. Viswanath b K. Ghavri	98	Ind	Bombay	1974–75
	NOT OUT	92	Pak	Lahore	1974–75
	c G.R. Viswanath b M. Amarnath	93	Ind	Bridgetown	1975–76
	c D.S. Steele b D.L. Underwood	97	Eng	Nottingham	1976
	c G.N. Yallop b W.M. Clark	92	Aus	Port-of-Sp.	1977–78
	b S. Venkataraghavan	98	Ind	Madras	1978–79
C.H. Lloyd	c A.P.E. Knott b D.L. Underwood	94	Eng	Birmingham	1973
	NOT OUT	91	Aus	Melbourne	1975–76
	c P.R. Downton b R.D. Jackman	95	Eng	Kingston	1980–81
C.G. Greenidge (on debut)	Run out	93	Ind	Bangalore	1974–75
	b Majid Khan	91	Pak	Georgetown	1976–77
	c Haroon Rashid b Imran Khan	96	Pak	Georgetown	1976–77
	c S.L. Boock b G.B. Troup	91	NZ	Christchurch	1979–80
	c W.K. Lees b G.B. Troup	97	NZ	Christchurch	1979–80
	c R.M. Hogg b G.F. Lawson	95	Aus	Adelaide	1984–85
K.D. Boyce	NOT OUT	95	Aus	Adelaide	1975–76
I.V.A. Richards	c G.S. Chappell b D.K. Lillee	98	Aus	Melbourne	1975–76
	c S. Mohammad b S. Nawaz	92	Pak	Bridgetown	1976–77
	c P.M. Toohey b G. Dymock	96	Aus	Melbourne	1979–80
S.F.A.F. Bacchus	b B.S. Bedi	96	Ind	Bangalore	1978–79

Batsman	How out		Opp.	Venue	Season
H.A. Gomes	c S. Gavaskar b S. Venkataraghavan	91	Ind	Madras	1978–79
	NOT OUT	90	Eng	Kingston	1980–81
	NOT OUT	92	Eng	Lord's	1984
D.L. Haynes	c & b J.E. Emburey	96	Eng	Port-of-Sp.	1980–81
	c Kapil Dev b R.J. Shastri	92	Ind	Bridgetown	1982–83
	b R.J. Hadlee	90	NZ	Georgetown	1984–85
M.D. Marshall	c & b Kapil Dev	92	Ind	Kanpur	1983–84
P.J. Dujon	c Kapil Dev b R.J. Shastri	98	Ind	Ahmedabad	1983–84
A.L. Logie	b T.G. Hogan	97	Aus	Port-of-Sp.	1983–84
	NOT OUT	95	Eng	Lord's	1988
	c S.R. Waugh b T.B.A. May	93	Aus	Perth	1988–89
	c A.J. Lamb b A.R.C. Fraser	98	Eng	Port–of–Sp.	1989–90
R.B. Richardson	c N.S. Sidhu b Arshad Ayub	93	Ind	Bridgetown	1988–89
	b Kapil Dev	99	Ind	Port-of-Sp.	1988–89
	lbw b M.E. Waugh	99	Aus	Bridgetown	1990–91
B.C. Lara	b Asfif Mujtaba	96	Pak	Port-of-Sp.	1992–93
J.C. Adams	NOT OUT	95	Eng	Kingston	1993–94
New Zealand					
R.C. Blunt	b R.W. Robins	96	Eng	Lord's	1931
W.A. Hadlee	hit wicket b A.W. Wellard	93	Eng	Manchester	1937
F.B. Smith	c D.C.S. Compton b W.J. Edrich	96	Eng	Leeds	1949
J.R. Reid	c D.V.P. Wright b J.C. Laker	93	Eng	The Oval	1949
	c H.D. Bromfield b A.H. McKinnon	92	SAf	Cape Town	1961–62
	b Arif Butt	97	Pak	Wellington	1964–65
J.E.F. Beck	Run out	99	SAf	Cape Town	1953–54
N.S. Harford (on debut)	c M. Ahmed b Khan Mohammad	93	Pak	Lahore	1955–56
J.W. Guy	lbw b S.P. Gupte	91	Ind	Calcutta	1955–56
R.W. Morgan	c & b Mufassirul Huq	97	Pak	Christchurch	1964–65
B.A.G. Murray	c Shafaq Rana b Parvez Sajjad	90	Pak	Lahore	1969–70
G.M. Turner	b G.S. Sobers	95	WI	Port-of-Sp.	1971–72
	lbw b G.G. Arnold	98	Eng	Christchurch	1974–75
M.G. Burgess	lbw b Madan Lal	95	Ind	Wellington	1975–76

Batsman	How out		Opp.	Venue	Season
R.W. Anderson (on debut)	c Majid Khan b M. Mohammad	92	Pak	Lahore	1976–77
G.P. Howarth	c P.H. Edwards b I.T. Botham	94	Eng	The Oval	1978
J.G. Wright	c R.G.D. Willis b N.G. Cowans	93	Eng	Leeds	1983
	c G.C. Dyer b C.J. McDermott	99	Aus	Melbourne	1987–88
	c A.J. Stewart b G.C. Small	98	Eng	Lord's	1990
	st R.C. Russell b P.C.R. Tufnell	99	Eng	Christchurch	1991–92
R.J. Hadlee	NOT OUT	92	Eng	Nottingham	1983
	c R.W. Taylor b R.G.D. Willis	99	Eng	Christchurch	1983–84
J.V. Coney	c R. de Alvis b A. Amarsinghe	92	SL	Colombo	1983–84
	c B.A. Reid b S.R. Waugh	98	Aus	Christchurch	1985–86
	c A.R. Border b C.J. McDermott	93	Aus	Auckland	1985–86
J.F. Reid	c Iqbal Qasim b Azeem Hafeez	97	Pak	Karachi	1984–85
M.J. Greatbach	NOT OUT	90	Ind	Hyderabad	1988–89
D.N. Patel	Run out	99	Eng	Christchurch	1991–92
M.D. Crowe	b C.J. McDermott	98	Aus	Wellington	1992–93
S.P. Fleming (on debut)	c Kapil Dev b R.K. Chauhan	92	Ind	Hamilton	1993–94

India

Batsman	How out		Opp.	Venue	Season
V. Mankad	Run out	96	WI	Port-of-Sp.	1952–53
V.L. Manjrekar	c A.R. MacGibbon b J.R. Reid	90	NZ	Calcutta	1955–56
	c B.R. Knight b D.A. Allen	96	Eng	Kanpur	1961–62
Pankaj Roy	c & b W.W. Hall	90	WI	Bombay	1958–59
	c R. Benaud b L. Kline	99	Aus	Delhi	1959–60
N.J. Contractor	lbw b W.W. Hall	92	WI	Delhi	1958–59
	c & b Intikkhab Alam	92	Pak	Delhi	1960–61
C.G. Borde	hit wicket b R. Gilchrist	96	WI	Delhi	1958–59
	b W.W. Hall	93	WI	Kingston	1961–62
M.L. Jaisimha	Run out	99	Pak	Kanpur	1960–61
S.A. Durani	c J.G. Binks b J.S.E. Price	90	Eng	Bombay	1963–64
Hanumant Singh	c N.C. O'Neill b T.R. Veivers	94	Aus	Madras	1964–65

Batsman	How out		Opp.	Venue	Season
F.M. Engineer	c V. Pollard b B.W. Yuile	90	NZ	Madras	1964–65
A.L. Wadekar	c D.B. Close b R. Illingworth	91	Eng	Leeds	1967
	c A.P. Sheahan b R.B. Simpson	99	Aus	Melbourne	1967–68
	NOT OUT	91	Aus	Delhi	1969–70
	c K.W.R. Fletcher b A.W. Greig	90	Eng	Kanpur	1972–73
R.F. Surti	c M.G. Burgess b G.A. Bartlett	99	NZ	Auckland	1967–68
Mansur Pataudi	c W.M. Lawry b J.W. Gleeson	95	Aus	Bombay	1969–70
A.V. Mankad	c K.D. Walters b A.A. Mallett	97	Aus	Delhi	1969–70
G.R. Viswanath	NOT OUT	97	WI	Madras	1974–75
	c R.C. Fredericks b L.R. Gibbs	95	WI	Bombay	1974–75
	c K.J. Wright b B. Yardley	96	Aus	Calcutta	1979–80
M. Amarnath	c J.B. Gannon b J.R. Thomson	90	Aus	Perth	1977–78
	c P.J. Dujon b M.D. Marshall	91	WI	Bridgetown	1982–83
	c N.G. Cowans b N.A. Foster	95	Eng	Madras	1984–85
S.M. Gavaskar	c Sarfraz Nawaz b M. Mohammad	97	Pak	Lahore	1978–79
	c C.H. Lloyd b M.A. Holding	90	WI	Ahmedabad	1983–84
	c D.M. Jones b R.J. Bright	90	Aus	Madras	1986–87
	c Tauseef Ahmed b Abdul Qadir	91	Pak	Madras	1986–87
	c Rizwan–uz–Zasman b I. Qasim	96	Pak	Bangalore	1986–87
C.P.S. Chauhan	c Wasim Bari b Javed Miandad	93	Pak	Lahore	1978–79
	c R.W. Marsh b D.K. Lillee	97	Aus	Adelaide	1980–81
R.J. Shastri	lbw b G.A. Gooch	93	Eng	Delhi	1981–82
Kapil Dev	c P.J.W. Allott b P.H. Edwards	97	Eng	The Oval	1982
	lbw b M.A. Holding	98	WI	St John's	1982–83
D.B. Vengsarkar	Run out	90	SL	Madras	1982–83
	c W.W. Davis b M.D. Marshall	94	WI	St John's	1982–83
	NOT OUT	98	SL	Colombo	1985–86
	st Salim Yousuf b Tauseef Ahmed	96	Pak	Madras	1986–87
Arun Lal	b C.A. Walsh	93	WI	Calcutta	1987–88
K. Srikkanth	c T.J. Franklin b Arshad Ayub	94	NZ	Bombay	1988–89
N.S. Sidhu	c Imran Khan b Zakir Khan	97	Pak	Sialkot	1989–90
	lbw b M. Muralidharan	99	SL	Bangalore	1993–94
	c A.C. Parore b M.N. Hart	98	NZ	Hamilton	1993–94
W.V. Raman	c A.H. Jones b D.K. Morrison	96	NZ	Christchurch	1989–90
M. Prabhakar	c I.D.S. Smith b R.J. Hadlee	95	NZ	Napier	1989–90

Batsman	How out		Opp.	Venue	Season
M. Prabhakar	c H.P. Tillekaratne b R.S. Kalpage	95	SL	Colombo	1993–94
S.V. Manjrekar	c R.A. Smith b E.E. Hemmings	93	Eng	Manchester	1990
S.R. Tendulkar	b S.D. Anurasiri	96	SL	Bangalore	1993–94
Pakistan					
Hanif Mohammad	c(sub) b V. Mankad	96	Ind	Bombay	1952–53
	st B.N. Jarman b T.R. Veivers	93	Aus	Melbourne	1964–65
Waqar Hassan	b G.S. Ramchand	97	Ind	Calcutta	1952–53
Maqsood Ahmed	st N.S. Tamhane b S.P. Gupte	99	Ind	Lahore	1954–55
A.H. Kardar	st N.S. Tamhane b S.P. Gupte	93	Ind	Karachi	1954–55
Imtiaz Ahmed	lbw b R. Gilchrist	91	WI	Bridgetown	1957–58
	c M.C. Cowdrey b J.D.F. Larter	98	Eng	The Oval	1962
Wazir Mohammad	NOT OUT	97	WI	Georgetown	1957–58
Saeed Ahmed	c F.C.M. Alexander b J. Taylor	97	WI	Port–of–Sp.	1957–58
	c R.N. Harvey b R.R. Lindwall	91	Aus	Karachi	1959–60
Abdul Kadir (on debut)	Run out	95	Aus	Karachi	1964–65
Shafqat Rana	c B.F. Hastings b D.R. Hadlee	95	NZ	Lahore	1969–70
Asif Iqbal	c K.J. Wadsworth b H.J. Howarth	92	NZ	Dacca	1969–70
Sadiq Mohammad	c & b B.L. d'Oliveira	91	Eng	Leeds	1971
	NOT OUT	98	WI	Karachi	1974–75
	c J.M. Brearley b I.T. Botham	97	Eng	Leeds	1978
Majid Khan	c D.L. Amiss b P.I. Pocock	99	Eng	Karachi	1972–73
	b D.L. Underwood	98	Eng	The Oval	1974
	st W.K. Lees b D.R. O'Sullivan	98	NZ	Hyderabad	1976–77
	c D.L. Murray b C.E.H. Croft	92	WI	Port–of–Sp.	1976–77
Mushtaq Mohammad	Run out	99	Eng	Karachi	1972–73
Zaheer Abbas	b G.J. Gilmour	90	Aus	Melbourne	1976–77
	c C.P.S. Chauhan b S.M. Gavaskar	96	Ind	Faisalabad	1978–79
	c & b B. Yardley	90	Aus	Melbourne	1981–82
	c R.W. Marsh b G.F. Lawson	91	Aus	Karachi	1982–83
Wasim Raja	lbw b Kapil Dev	97	Ind	Delhi	1979–80
	NOT OUT	94	Ind	Kanpur	1979–80

Batsman	How out		Opp.	Venue	Season
Taslim Arif (on debut)	c C.P.S. Chauhan b Kapil Dev	90	Ind	Calcutta	1979–80
Mudassar Nazar	c D.K. Lillee b B. Yardley	95	Aus	Melbourne	1981–82
Javed Miandad	st H.M. Goonatillake b D.S. deSilva	92	SL	Karachi	1981–82
	c(sub) b Madan Lal	99	Ind	Bangalore	1983–84
	Run out	94	Ind	Madras	1986–87
	b M.L. Sua	92	NZ	Hamilton	1992–93
Mohsin Khan	c M. Amarnath b Madan Lal	94	Ind	Lahore	1982–83
	lbw b Kapil Dev	91	Ind	Karachi	1982–83
Sarfraz Nawaz	c M.W. Gatting b C.L. Smith	90	Eng	Lahore	1983–84
Qasim Omar	c J.J. Crowe b J.V. Coney	96	NZ	Dunedin	1984–85
Salim Malik	c D.I. Gower b P.H. Edmonds	99	Eng	Leeds	1987
Salim Yousuf	NOT OUT	91	Eng	Birmingham	1987
Aamer Malik	NOT OUT	98	Eng	Lord's	1987–88
Shoaib Mohammad	b S.R. Waugh	94	Aus	Karachi	1988–89
	lbw b Kapil Dev	95	Ind	Karachi	1989–90
Ramiz Raja	c H.P. Tillekeratne b S.D. Anurasiri	98	SL	Sialkot	1991–92
Imran Khan	NOT OUT	93	SL	Sialkot	1991–92
Basit Ali	NOT OUT	92	WI	Bridgetown	1992–93

Sri Lanka

Batsman	How out		Opp.	Venue	Season
R.L. Dias	c Salim Malik b Iqbal Qasim	98	Pak	Faisalabad	1981–82
	c S.M. Gavaskar b R.C. Shukla	97	Ind	Madras	1982–83
	c S. Viswanath b Chetan Sharma	95	Ind	Colombo	1985–86
R.S. Madugalle	NOT OUT	91	Pak	Faisalabad	1981–82
A. Ranatunga	c D.K. Lillee b B. Yardley	90	Aus	Kandy	1982–83
S. Wettimuny	b T.G. Hogan	96	Aus	Kandy	1982–83
L.R.D. Mendis	c G. Fowler b I.T. Botham	94	Eng	Lord's	1984
J.R. Ratnayeke	lbw b Kapil Dev	93	Ind	Kanpur	1986–87
P.A. de Silva	c I.D.S. Smith b C.L. Cairns	96	NZ	Auckland	1990–91
	c M. Azharuddin b A. Kumble	93	Ind	Colombo	1993–94
H.P. Tillekaratne	c A.C. Parore b G.E. Bradburn	93	NZ	Colombo	1992–93
	NOT OUT	93	Eng	Colombo	1992–93

Batsman	How out		Opp.	Venue	Season
H.P. Tillekaratne	lbw b B.N. Schultz	92	SAf	Moratuwa	1993–94
Zimbabwe					
G.W. Flower	lbw b Maninder Singh	96	Ind	Delhi	1992–93

'SUPER NINETIES' IN TEST CRICKET
(scores of 190–199, 290–299)

Score	Batsman	Match	Venue	Season
299*	D.G. Bradman	Aus v. SAf	Adelaide	1931–32
299	M.D. Crowe	NZ v. SL	Wellington	1990–91
291	I.V.A. Richards	WI v. Eng	The Oval	1976
199	Mudassar Nazar	Pak v. Ind	Faisalabad	1984–85
199	M. Azharuddin	Ind v. SL	Kanpur	1986–87
198*	A.L. Hassett	Aus v. Ind	Adelaide	1947–48
198	G.S. Sobers	WI v. Ind	Kanpur	1958–59
197*	F.M.M. Worrell	WI v. Eng	Bridgetown	1959–60
197	E.D. Weekes	WI v. Pak	Bridgetown	1957–58
196	G.B. Legge	Eng v. NZ	Auckland	1929–30
196	L. Hutton	Eng v. WI	Lord's	1939
196	A.R. Morris	Aus v. Eng	The Oval	1948
196	I.M. Chappell	Aus v. Pak	Adelaide	1972–73
196	A.R. Border	Aus v. Eng	Lord's	1985
196	G.A. Gooch	Eng v. Aus	The Oval	1985
195	C. Washbrook	Eng v. SAf	Johannesburg	1948–49
194	H. Sutcliffe	Eng v. Aus	Sydney	1932–33
194	E.D. Weekes	WI v. Ind	Bombay	1948–49
194	C.G. Greenidge	WI v. Ind	Kanpur	1983–84
194	R.B. Richardson	WI v. Ind	Georgetown	1988–89
193*[a]	W. Bardsley	Aus v. Eng	Lord's	1926
192*	I.V.A. Richards	WI v. Ind	Delhi	1974–75
192	B.K. Kunderan	Ind v. Eng	Madras	1963–64
192	I.M. Chappell	Aus v. Eng	The Oval	1975
192	M. Azharuddin	Ind v. NZ	Auckland	1989–90
191*[a]	F.M.M. Worrell	WI v. Eng	Nottingham	1957
191	C. Hill	Aus v. SAf	Sydney	1910–11
191	W.J. Edrich	Eng v. SAf	Manchester	1947
191	G. Boycott	Eng v. Aus	Leeds	1977
190	R.N. Harvey	Aus v. SAf	Sydney	1952–53
190	S. Wettimuny	SL v. Eng	Lord's	1984
190*[a]	A.J. Stewart	Eng v. Pak	Birmingham	1992

* = not out
[a] = carried his bat

99–RUN PARTNERSHIPS IN TEST CRICKET

Wkt no.	Batsmen	Match	Venue	Season
First	C.C. Hunte & M.R. Bynoe	WI v. Ind	Madras	1966–67
	R.B. Simpson & W.M. Lawry	Aus v. Ind	Adelaide	1967–68
	Sadiq Mohammad & Talat Ali	Pak v. Eng	Lahore	1972–73
	D.L. Haynes & P.V. Simmons	WI v. SAf	Bridgetown	1991–92
	R. Mahanama&U. Hathurusinghe	SL v. Eng	Colombo	1992–93
Second	C.S. Dempster & G.L. Weir	NZ v. Eng	Lord's	1931
	A.R. Morris & D.G. Bradman[a]	Aus v. Eng	Adelaide	1946–47
	W.E. Russell & P.H. Parfitt	Eng v. SAf	The Oval	1965
	B.C. Broad & R.T. Robinson	Eng v. Aus	Sydney	1987–88
Third	J.B. Hobbs & K.L. Hutchings	Eng v. Aus	Melbourne	1907–08
	L. Hutton & M.C. Cowdrey	Eng v. Aus	Adelaide	1954–55
	A. Bacher & E.J. Barlow	SAf v. Eng	Notting'm	1965
	C. Greenidge & A. Kallicharran	WI v. Pak	Georgetown	1976–77
	S. Amarnath & G.R. Viswanath	Ind v. Pak	Lahore	1978–79
	J.F. Reid & G.P. Howarth	NZ v. Ind	Wellington	1980–81
	R.B. Richardson & P.J.L. Dujon	WI v. Aus	Melbourne	1988–89
	A.H. Jones & M.D. Crowe	NZ v. Aus	Perth	1993–94
Fourth	C.J. Barnett & M. Leyland	Eng v. Aus	Brisbane	1936–37
	R.N. Harvey & K.R. Miller	Aus v. Eng	Adelaide	1950–51
	N.C. O'Neill & L.E. Favell	Aus v. Pak	Lahore	1959–60
	C.C. Hunte & S.M. Nurse	WI v. Eng	Manchester	1966
	S.M. Gavaskar & G.R. Viswanath	Ind v. WI	Port–of–Sp.	1970–71
	C.G. Greenidge & C.H. Lloyd	WI v. Eng	Lord's	1976
	S.M. Kirmani & D.Vengsarkar	Ind v. Aus	Madras	1979–80
	J.G. Wright & J.V. Coney	NZ v. Ind	Auckland	1980–81
	R.L. Dias & L.R.D. Mendis	SL v. Ind	Colombo	1985–86
	M.A. Taylor & D.M. Jones	Aus v. Eng	Leeds	1989
Fifth	T.W. Hayward & G.H. Hirst	Eng v. Aus	Sydney	1903–04
	H.W. Taylor & R.H. Catterall	SAf v. Eng	Leeds	1924
	K.J. Viljoen & H.B. Cameron	SAf v. Eng	Manchester	1935
	F.M.M. Worrell & G.E. Gomez	WI v. Eng	Port–of–Sp.	1947–48
	A.L. Hassett & S.J.E. Loxton	Aus v. SAf	Port Eliz.	1949–50
	R.B. Kanhai & O.G. Smith	WI v. Pak	Port–of–Sp.	1957–58
	G.S. Chappell & G.J. Cosier	Aus v. WI	Sydney	1975–76
	B. Yardley & K.J. Hughes	Aus v. Ind	Bangalore	1979–80
	R.S. Madugalle & A. Ranatunge	SL v. Eng	Colombo	1981–82
	D.I. Gower & A.J. Stewart	Eng v. Aus	Sydney	1990–91
	D.J. Cullinan & J.N. Rhodes	SAf v. Ind	Cape Town	1992–93
	P. A. de Silva & H. Tillekeratne	SL v. Ind	Colombo	1993–94
Sixth	G.A. Faulkner & S.J. Snooke	SAf v. Eng	J'burg	1909–10

Wkt no.	Batsmen	Match	Venue	Season
	W.A. Hadlee & M.L. Page	NZ v. Eng	Manchester	1937
	A.R. Border & I.A. Healy	Aus v. NZ	Christchurch	1992–93
Eighth	P.H. Parfitt & D.A. Allen	Eng v. Pak	Leeds	1962

[a] = unbroken partnership

NINETIES IN FIRST-CLASS CRICKET

HIGHEST SCORE OF 99 NOT OUT
(list perhaps not complete)

Batsman	Opponent	Venue	Season
J. Evans (Kent)	MCC	Chislehurst	1823
G. Anderson (Yorkshire)	Nottinghamshire	Nottingham	1864
R.T. Crawford (Leicestershire)	Worcestershire	Leicester	1902
G.W. Hodgkinson (Somerset)	Gloucestershire	Taunton	1910
R.O. Lagden (Oxford Uni.)	Leveson–Gower XI	Eastbourne	1912
J.J. Bridges (Somerset)	Essex	Weston–super–mare	1919
K.A. Saeed (Punjab 'B')	Punjab	Lahore	1957–58
G.A. Bartlett (Central Distr.)	Auckland	Auckland	1959–60
K.J. O'Keeffe (Australians)	Auckland	Auckland	1973–74
W.K. Watson[a] (Eastern Prov.)	North Transvaal	Port Elizabeth	1982–83
R.L. Ollis (Somerset)	Gloucestershire	Bristol	1983
G.K. Robertson[a] (Central Dist.)	Otago	Oamaru	1985–86
Jamal Siddiqi[a] (Rawalpindi)	Habib Bank	Lahore	1987–88

[a] = Current player

Note: Bridges added 143 runs in 70 minutes for 10th wicket with A.H.D. Gibbs—still a county record; Bartlett added 133 for the last wicket with I.A. Colquhoun who was run out; Robertson added 115 for the 9th wicket, then last man was out for 0; Watson added 151 for the 9th wicket, then last man run out for 0; O'Keeffe is the only Australian in the list.

NINETIES IN LIMITED–OVER INTERNATIONALS

In the 25 year history of limited–over internationals (LOI), 111 (Nelson's number!) nineties have been recorded. The Australian batsmen have made most nineties, 24: followed by West Indian and Indian batsmen, 17 each; English bats, 15; Pakistanis, 14; New Zealanders, 13; South Africans, 6; and Sri Lankans, 5. Batsmen from

Zimbabwe, United Arab Emirates (UAE), Canada, East Africa and Bangladesh have not recorded a ninety yet.

Dean Jones (Australia) and Martin Crowe (New Zealand) have hit most LOI nineties, 6 each; followed by Richie Richardson (West Indies) and Kris Srikkanth (India), 5 each; and Allan Border (Australia), Alan Lamb (England) and Mohammad Azharuddin (India), 4 each. England's John Edrich was the first to hit a LOI ninety (90 v. India, 1974) and another Englishman, Geoff Boycott, was the first to record a LOI 99 (v. Australia in 1980). Bruce Edgar of New Zealand, Dean Jones and Richie Richardson were unfortunate to remain 99 not out. Below is a complete list of batsmen making nineties in LOI:

Score	Batsman	Match	Venue	Season
99	G. Boycott	Eng v. Aus	The Oval	1980
99*	B.A. Edgar	NZ v. Ind	Auckland	1980–81
99	A.J. Lamb	Eng v. Ind	The Oval	1982
99	K. Srikkanth	Ind v. Eng	Cuttack	1984–85
99*	D.M. Jones	Aus v. SL	Adelaide	1984–85
99*	R.B. Richardson	WI v. Pak	Sharjah, UAE	1985–86
99	B.C. Broad	Eng v. Pak	The Oval	1987
99	Rameez Raja	Pak v. Eng	Karachi	1987–88
98*	C.G. Greenidge	WI v. Eng	Sydney	1979–80
98	K.J. Hughes	Aus v. Eng	Birmingham	1980
98*	G.M. Wood	Aus v. Ind	Melbourne	1980–81
98	I.V.A. Richards	WI v. SL	Brisbane	1984–85
98	R.S. Mahanama	SL v. Ind	Bombay	1986–87
98	N.S. Sidhu	Ind v. WI	Sharjah, UAE	1991–92
98	Zahid Fazal	Pak v. Ind	Sharjah, UAE	1991–92
98	D.M. Jones	Aus v. SAf	Brisbane	1993–94
98	A. Ranatunga	SL v. Ind	Hyderabad	1993–94
97	Zaheer Abbas	Pak v. SL	Nottingham	1975
97	I.V.A. Richards	WI v. Eng	Lord's	1976
97	D.L. Haynes	WI v. Ind	Port–of–Spain	1982–83
97	M.D. Crowe	NZ v. Eng	The Oval	1983
97*	A.J. Lamb	Eng v. NZ	Auckland	1983–84
97	B.C. Broad	Eng v. Pak	Perth	1986–87
97	D.M. Wellham	Aus v. Eng	Sydney	1986–87
97	P.N. Kirsten	SAf v. NZ	Brisbane	1993–94
97	W.J. Cronje	SAf v. Aus	Verwoerdburg	1993–94
96	M.W. Gatting	Eng v. Aus	Birmingham	1981
96	C.G. Greenidge	WI v. Ind	Indore	1983–84
96	R.H. Vance	NZ v. SL	Sharjah, UAE	1987–88

Score	Batsman	Match	Venue	Season
96	P.A. de Silva	SL v. Aus	Margoa	1989–90
96	D.L. Haynes	WI v. Pak	Sydney	1992–93
95	R.B. McCosker	Aus v. WI	Sydney	1979–80
95*	Zaheer Abbas	Pak v. WI	Sialkot	1980–81
95	K. Srikkanth	Ind v. SL	Delhi	1982–83
95*	I.V.A. Richards	WI v. Aus	Lord's	1983
95	Mudassar Nazar	Pak v. Aus	Sharjah, UAE	1985–86
95*	D.B. Vengsarkar	Ind v. Pak	Sharjah, UAE	1986–87
95	W.V. Raman	Ind v. WI	Rajkot	1987–88
95*	M. Azharuddin	Ind v. Eng	Gwalior	1992–93
95*	B.C. Lara	WI v. Pak	Port–of–Spain	1992–93
94	G.A. Gooch	Eng v. NZ	Scarborough	1978
94	A.J. Lamb	Eng v. Aus	Melbourne	1982–83
94	G.M. Turner	NZ v. Eng	Wellington	1982–83
94*	D.B. Vengsarkar	Ind v. Pak	Sialkot	1984–85
94	G.R. Marsh	Aus v. WI	Adelaide	1986–87
94	R.B. Richardson	WI v. Aus	Georgetown	1990–91
94	M.A. Taylor	Aus v. SL	Colombo	1992–93
94	M.D. Crowe	NZ v. Zim	Harare	1992–93
93	Zaheer Abbas	Pak v. WI	The Oval	1979
93*	M. Azharuddin	Ind v. Pak	Melbourne	1984–85
93*	K. Srikkanth	Ind v. Aus	Melbourne	1984–85
93*	M.D. Crowe	NZ v. Eng	Manchester	1986
93	G.R. Marsh	Aus v. Eng	Brisbane	1986–87
93	D.M. Jones	Aus v. Eng	Melbourne	1986–87
93	R.B. Richardson	WI v. Eng	Jaipur	1987–88
93	D.C. Boon	Aus v. Zim	Cuttack	1987–88
93*	D.M. Jones	Aus v. WI	Sydney	1988–89
93	J.G. Wright	NZ v. Ban[a]	Sharjah, UAE	1989–90
93	A.H. Jones	NZ v. Ban	Sharjah, UAE	1989–90
93*	D.L. Haynes	WI v. Pak	Melbourne	1991–92
93	M. Azharuddin	Ind v. Aus	Brisbane	1991–92
93	A.C. Hudson	SAf v. Pak	Durban	1992–93
92	G.S. Chapell	Aus v. Eng	Melbourne	1979–80
92	K. Srikkanth	Ind v. SL	Bangalore	1982–83
92*	D.I. Gower	Eng v. NZ	Birmingham	1983
92	K.C. Wessels	Aus v. Pak	Sydney	1983–84
92*	R.B. Richardson	WI v. Pak	Rawalpindi	1985–86
92*	S.M. Gavaskar	Ind v. Aus	Sydney	1985–86
92	S.M. Gavaskar	Ind v. Pak	Sharjah, UAE	1985–86
92	K. Srikkanth	Ind v. SL	Sharjah, UAE	1986–87
92	G.A. Gooch	Eng v. WI	Jaipur	1987–88

Score	Batsman	Match	Venue	Season
92	D.M. Jones	Aus v. NZ	Perth	1987–88
92*	D.C. Boon	Aus v. NZ	Sharjah, UAE	1989–90
92	R.S. Mahanama	SL v. Ind	Colombo	1993–94
92	P.V. Simmons	WI v. SL	Sharjah, UAE	1993–94
91*	B.M. Laird	Aus v. Pak	Lahore	1982–83
91	G.M. Wood	Aus v. NZ	Melbourne	1982–83
91*	Javed Miandad	Pak v. SL	Lahore	1985–86
91	G.A. Gooch	Eng v. NZ	Manchester	1986
91*	A.R. Border	Aus v. Ind	Rajkot	1986–87
91	A.R. Border	Aus v. Eng	Adelaide	1986–87
91	A.J. Lamb	Eng v. Ind	Kanpur	1989–90
91*	Salim Malik	Pak v. WI	Lahore	1990–91
91	Aamir Sohail	Pak v. Ind	Sharjah, UAE	1991–92
91	R.A. Smith	Eng v. Ind	Perth	1991–92
91	M.D. Crowe	NZ v. Pak	Auckland	1991–92
91	A.J. Stewart	Eng v. Ind	Jaipur	1992–93
91*	M.D. Crowe	NZ v. Aus	Wellington	1992–93
91	M.D. Crowe	NZ v. Aus	Hamilton	1992–93
91	M. Prabhakar	Ind v. Zim	Indore	1993–94
91*	W.J. Cronje	SAf v. Aus	Melbourne	1993–94
90	J.H. Edrich	Eng v. Ind	Leeds	1974
90	G.S. Chappell	Aus v. NZ	Melbourne	1980–81
90	S.M. Gavaskar	Ind v. WI	Berbice	1982–83
90	C.G. Greenidge	WI v. Aus	Lord's	1983
90	A.R. Border	Aus v. WI	Castries	1983–84
90*	Javed Miandad	Pak v. NZ	Hamilton	1984–85
90*	A.R. Border	Aus v. Ind	Srinagar	1986–87
90	A.H. Jones	NZ v. Eng	Auckland	1987–88
90	Aamir Malik	Pak v. Aus	Perth	1988–89
90	R.B. Richardson	WI v. Aus	Port–of–Spain	1990–91
90	Rameez Raja	Pak v. WI	Sharjah, UAE	1991–92
90	K.C. Wessels	SAf v. Ind	Delhi	1991–92
90	P.N. Kirsten	SAf v. NZ	Auckland	1991–92
90	D.M. Jones	Aus v. Ind	Brisbane	1991–92
90	Inzamam–ul–Haq	Pak v. Zim	Sharjah, UAE	1992–93
90	A.P. Gurusinha	SL v. Pak	Sharjah, UAE	1992–93
90*	Inzamam–ul–Haq	Pak v. WI	Port–of–Spain	1992–93
90*	P.V. Simmons	WI v. SL	Sharjah, UAE	1993–94
90	M. Azharuddin	Ind v. SAf	Calcutta	1993–94
90	S.P. Fleming	NZ v. Ind	Napier	1993–94

* = not out
Ban = Bangladesh

Index